Studies in American Popular History and Culture

Edited by

Jerome Nadelhaft
University of Maine

A Routledge Series

STUDIES IN AMERICAN POPULAR HISTORY AND CULTURE

JEROME NADELHAFT, *General Editor*

WOMEN WORKERS ON STRIKE
Narratives of Southern Women Unionists

Roxanne Newton

Routledge
Taylor & Francis Group
NEW YORK AND LONDON

Routledge
Taylor & Francis Group
711 Third Avenue,
New York, NY 10017

Routledge
Taylor & Francis Group
2 Park Square
Milton Park, Abingdon
Oxon, OX14 4RN

© 2007 by Taylor & Francis Group, LLC
Routledge is an imprint of Taylor & Francis Group, an Informa business

Transferred to Digital Printing 2008

First issued in paperback 2012

International Standard Book Number-13: 978-0-415-98147-7 (Hardcover)
International Standard Book Number-13: 978-0-415-65330-5 (Paperback)

Library of Congress Cataloging-in-Publication Data

Newton, Roxanne.
    Women workers on strike : narratives of southern women unionists / Roxanne Newton.
        p. cm. -- (Studies in American popular history and culture)
    Includes bibliographical references and index.
    ISBN 0-415-98147-6 (alk. paper)
    1. Women labor union members--Southern States--History. 2. Feminism--Southern States--History. 3. Strikes and lockouts--Southern States--History. 4. Labor unions--Southern States--History. 5. Women--Employment--Southern States. 6. Sex discrimination in employment--Southern States. I. Title.

HD6079.2.S644N48 2006
331.4'792975--dc22   2006022438

Visit the Taylor & Francis Web site at
http://www.taylorandfrancis.com

and the Routledge Web site at
http://www.routledge-ny.com

*To Michael Allen Morrison for his unwavering encouragement,
valuable insights, and abiding love;
and to the women unionists in this study
for their courageous dedication to workplace democracy and
women's equality*

Contents

Contents

Acknowledgments

I am indebted to James Andrews, president of the North Carolina State AFL-CIO, who provided information about women unionists in the state and offered early direction to this project. I am also indebted to Robert Anthony and the staff of the North Carolina Collection at UNC Chapel Hill for information and materials regarding unions and strikes, and I am grateful to Sherry Linkon and John Russo at the Center for Working-Class Studies at Youngstown State University for their encouragement and for the important work that they do every day.

I wish to thank Julian Mason whose friendship and guidance through the years have been important in my development as a scholar. I am also grateful to Tricia Hayes and Michael Jenkins for their friendship and support, and to Kathleen Casey, Hepzibah Roskelly, Svi Shapiro, and Leila Villaverde at UNC Greensboro for their invaluable insights. I also wish to thank my colleagues at Mitchell Community College for their unfailing encouragement and friendship.

Finally, I am deeply grateful to my mother and father, Joan and Vernon Newton, who gave me the gifts of wonder, confidence, and persistence; and to my children, Ethan and Hannah Miller, who inspire me with their hopes and dreams.

Chapter One
The Fabric of Hope and Resistance

Gender, class, and culture in the working lives of Southern women are threaded onto the loom of history as intricately woven patterns of resistance to oppression and exploitation. However, the shuttles are often stilled before the cloth is made. In historical representation, the lived experiences of working-class women in the South emerge as slubs on remnants, the forgotten, unused fabric of the ages. Museums and bookshelves are bereft; the cold (man's) history of humanity lacks the warmth of working women's stories. Their narratives are woven in their secret tapestries of Self and folded and stored in the dusty closets of Anonymity. This study endeavors to give women the necessary tools of voice, agency, and power—their spindles, threads, and shuttles—to spin, weave, and craft their narratives of protest, resistance, hope, and transcendence.

The voices of women organizing, working, and striking alongside men in labor disputes have been neglected, overlooked, shut out, or shouted down. This collection of narratives attempts to restore the sounds of women's voices to the common chorus of united people in protest, re-threading the shuttles of truth and power in the loom of justice. The voices of these working-class women speak back to the dominant voices of capitalism and patriarchy. Employing narrative research methodology, this study involves North Carolina women from across the state who were interviewed about their experiences during strikes at their workplaces. Of various ages, races, and cultural backgrounds, these women were involved in strikes from 1934 to 2001. In addition, this study explores the ways that these women interpret their lived experiences from divergent perspectives within the context of their life narratives. In presenting their stories, I aim to preserve the women's language and the particular meanings they ascribe to their words, and hence, to their lives. In attending to their silences, selectivities, and slippages, I also note the various interpretations possible for each respondent.

The women who were interviewed worked, or continue to work, in industries as disparate as textile mills, telecommunications, tire manufacturing, and paper production. It should be noted that unions and strikes are rare in North Carolina, a so-called "Right-to-Work" state where government employees are banned from organizing, and workers in union plants are exempt from participation if they choose. Therefore, these women's voices are among the least liberated and the most silenced of working women in the United States, an oppression that begins, but does not end, with the legal institutions of the state that inhibit collective organizing and effective action. Feminist studies and working-class studies require additional research in order to piece together these women's stories into a collective quilt of agency and action, a coverlet of unity and power that may shelter the hopes of all working women, regardless of geography, ethnicity, or culture.

The discourse of working women involved in labor disputes adds volume to the diminishing voices of protest in a time when organized labor and the working class are struggling to be heard. Women's voices are needed to carry these cries of protest above the din sounding at the Wailing Wall of American Capitalism. Using the excuses of a depressed economy, global terrorism, and transnational trade, increasingly powerful corporations and the employing class have effectively suppressed organized labor and workers' rights. The narratives of the women in this study highlight their role as active subjects whose life histories demonstrate their strength and determination. Their stories are capable of informing and enlightening all working women who are striving to speak in new transcendent voices, weaving a sustaining, durable cloth from which all members of the working class may craft their garments of hope and resistance.

These narratives also reflect southerners' experiences with organized labor in the region of the United States with the fewest union members. In addition, union participation in North Carolina is significant because the state has consistently maintained the lowest percentage of union members among all workers since the Department of Labor has been collecting data.[1] Nationally, only 12.5 percent of wage and salary workers in 2004 were union members, with North Carolinians' participation at 2.7 percent.[2] According to Timothy Minchin in *Fighting Against the Odds: A History of Southern Labor Since World War II*, "Antiunionism was written into North Carolina's laws, from its right-to-work act, passed shortly after Taft-Hartley, to a statute specifically forbidding collective bargaining with public employees."[3] Low union participation reflects the anti-union bias prevalent in the state even though unions are known to improve workers' conditions through increased wages, better benefits, and greater advocacy. Anti-union sentiment is also the result of the state's history of violent labor disputes. In 1929, workers in Gastonia and Marion were involved in strikes that became increasingly contentious and violent, often dividing families across the picket lines. The infamous 1929 Loray Mill Strike in Gaston County is emblematic of the unrest and violence in southern textile communities. In June of that year police officers attacked a small group of picketing strikers, mostly women and children, brutally beating a number of them. The strikers fled as quickly as they could, escaping to the union hall and the tent community. Soon thereafter, police officers arrived at the union hall. After an altercation, shots were fired. When the shooting was over, one union guard and four police officers were wounded, among them police chief Orville Aderholt, who died of his wounds the following day. Witnesses have conflicting accounts of the incident, so it is still unclear which group fired the first shots.[4]

Also in 1929 more than 1500 workers at the two largest mills in Marion walked off their jobs, protesting long hours and low pay, among other grievances.[5] The violence in Marion effectively quashed the union in that community, much as the earlier Gastonia dispute had done.

> Moreover, after an attempt to reopen the Clinchfield mill with strike-breakers failed, the National Guard was sent to Marion. There was little violence until . . . Clinchfield strikers prevented a non-union worker from moving into a house in the mill village and drove deputy sheriffs away with clubs and stones. Because of this, 74 strikers were arrested on the charge of "a rebellion against the constituted authority of the State of North Carolina."[6]

After a mediated agreement, the workers ended the strike. However, upon their return to work, they realized that the mill owners had reneged on the agreement, and nearly 250 of them again stopped work, resulting in an attack on the unarmed workers. Six of the workers were killed, and 18 others were wounded.[7]

In 1930, a prophetic essay entitled, "North Carolina at the Crossroads" by Nell Battle Lewis was published in the *Virginia Quarterly Review*. In a litany of conflicts, Lewis recounted the violent eruptions in Marion and Gastonia, among other disputes during the 1920s.

> Strikes in textile mills at Gastonia and Marion have resulted in eight homicides; three unrestrained demonstrations of mob lawlessness; three mobilizations of the militia; the State's most sensational and expensive trial in which twenty lawyers took part; more than three hundred

arrests involving numerous other court cases; eviction or planned eviction of more than a hundred families from their homes; and inflamma-
tion of public sentiment to a degree seldom equalled in the history of
the State.[8]

The disputes also attracted the attention of Sinclair Lewis who reported on
the Marion strike for Scripps-Howard Newspapers for national syndica-
tion. Sinclair later compiled the Marion articles in a booklet entitled, *Cheap
and Contented Labor: The Picture of a Southern Mill Town in 1929*. The
author described one striker thus: "I met a widow of 60 . . . . I was told
that she had no one to support her . . . . She had worked in the mill for
many years. 'But now,' said she, 'I can't go across the blood of our murdered boys at the mill gate. I don't know what is going to happen, but I
reckon it's time for the Lord to take care of me.'"[9] Lewis concluded that
the "Marion business men . . . will assist Capital to choke Labor."[10] A
reporter for the *Raleigh News and Observer* during the time of the strike,
Nell Battle Lewis later stated that the issue of labor divided the state, and
that "the question . . . vitally affects not only North Carolina but indirectly the South and the whole country. Only time can answer it."[11]

In 1958, a later generation of textile workers in Henderson, North
Carolina faced similar state-supported military opposition to the more than
one thousand strikers during a two-year dispute for improved working conditions. As in the Gastonia and Marion conflicts, the state brought in armed
militia to support company interests. "Large numbers of strikers were
arrested for disorderly conduct, assault, damaging personal property, and
violating the restraining order. Violence against strikers and union representatives by armed strikebreakers and others was ignored."[12] Three months
into the strike, the company brought in nonunion workers from nearby
Virginia, prompting violence, "including a bombing campaign that both
sides blamed on each other. The bombings attracted national press attention and provided ample ammunition to support employers' claims that
unions brought only discord and violence."[13] In Henderson, the once-suc-
cessful Textile Workers Union of America (TWUA) brought together black
and white workers and provided equally for the strikers' needs, regardless
of race. Women also assumed a major role in the strike, actively picketing
and speaking at rallies in cities outside the South. "The Henderson workers
sustained the strike for over two years in the face of the company's lock-
out and recruitment of strikebreakers, deployment of the Highway Patrol
and National Guard, and conviction of local union leaders on charges of
conspiracy to dynamite the plant."[14] Even today, the legacy of the state's
repression of unionists translates into fear and misunderstanding among

its citizens. During my research, I contacted the Henderson County Public Library to learn what materials and news articles were available, and I was told that documents related to the strike are repeatedly stolen, as if these thieves of history could somehow erase the truth about a time of social unrest and violence in their community.

While economic and social forces have opposed unionization in the South, religion also played a primary role. During some of the worst labor disputes in North Carolina, for example, religious leaders often sided with company owners during strikes while other ministers applauded their striking congregants for fighting the powerful enemies of the working people. "[S]o far as evidence is available, the place of the churches in the cultural fabric depended largely on the policies of the mills; lacking active cooperation of the mills, they tended to shrink in size and influence."[15] In Gaston County, ministers often were either outspoken against the union and the strike, or at least adopted a noncommittal stance. "Union organizers have consistently regarded ministers in Gaston County and in the South generally as among their worst enemies."[16]

In Marion during the 1929 strike, relationships between ministers and the union varied; workers belonged to several denominations, each of which responded to the strike differently. The "Methodist church, where the mill superintendent doubled as superintendent of the Sunday school," vehemently opposed the union and the strike.[17] However, the Baptist church, where the head deacon, Dan Elliott, was also a mill worker and strike leader, remained neutral until it replaced him with a mill supervisor when Elliott left to attend a labor college. The Baptist church then dismissed "twelve union members for 'unchristian conduct.'"[18] On the other hand, a mill worker was minister of an independent congregation formed by "a splinter group of Baptist workers" who supported the strike. The independent minister was "the only local minister to participate in the funerals of the men killed in the Marion strike."[19]

The Henderson strike of 1958 revealed an unusual and important confluence of religious values and union efforts, emphasizing that strikers were acting in accordance with their Christian beliefs. One common slogan from the dispute was "Jesus Leads Us, Cooper Needs Us, the Union Feeds Us," and letters to the editor of the Henderson newspaper reflected these three points. One letter writer suggested that John D. Cooper, the mill owner, was not a Christian man: "'If you love God, as much as you do your money, Henderson wouldn't be in the shape it is in tonight.'"[20] Another letter expressed hope that the union and management could reach an agreement: "If both parties were Christians, I sincerely believe a workable contract could be negotiated."[21] Religious leaders in Henderson were exceptional in their support of the striking workers; ministers in other mill villages felt they owed allegiance to their benefactors—the mill owners. Because of the anti-union bias inherent in social and religious networks in small towns across the region, southerners have been more likely to oppose organized labor.

The current environment in North Carolina reflects that opposition, with workers often failing to understand the value of collective bargaining and the workplace democracy that union participation affords. According to Stanley Aronowitz in *False Promises: The Shaping of the American Working Class Consciousness*, labor unions represent the "elementary organ of defense of their immediate economic interests" for workers and "their only weapons of defense against the deterioration of working conditions."[22] The women in this study, though few in number among the small group of unionists in North Carolina, provide insights into the benefits of union membership. I aim to highlight these women's experiences in order to share their stories about labor disputes and union empowerment. While at times in their narratives, these women's voices speak clearly and boldly, at other moments, their silences are more evident as they withhold ideas, emotions, and information. In the lived experiences of North Carolina women on strike, institutions, power relations, and individual and collective empowerment all play significant roles in determining the types of silences attributed to them.

The silences of women in this study reflect their various experiences. They live in communities across the state and work in different industries. Of varying ages and sensibilities, the respondents in this research share their experiences in narratives that reflect both their individuality and their collective understanding of their work and their world. To protect them from notoriety and possible retaliation, I refer to each of the respondents in this study by a pseudonym. Three of the women are former textile workers. Annie is a white retired textile employee in her eighties who still lives in her hometown, a community whose economy depended on the cotton mill. Though she crossed the picket lines as a teenager in the General Textile Strike of 1934, Annie was later fired for attempting to organize a Textile Workers Union of America (TWUA) local. Another former member of the TWUA, Katherine, also a white woman in her eighties, lives in another small town previously noted for textiles. Though she is retired, Katherine left the mill after the strike and never worked in textiles again. Joan is an African American woman in her fifties who is retired from textile work. She was a member of the International Ladies' Garment Workers Union (ILGWU) and the Union of Needletrades, Industrial, and Textile Employees (UNITE). She too still lives in her small hometown and works as a union business representative and volunteer in her community.

Five of the women in this study are former members of the Paper, Allied Chemical, and Energy (PACE) workers union. The paper mill where they worked closed in 2001 after a long stint as the major industry in their mountain county. All of the women are white and are retired or semi-retired. Camille, in her fifties, lives and works in the small county seat as a part-time bookkeeper. She is divorced and hopes to find full-time employment to augment her minimal retirement benefits, taken earlier than anticipated because of forced retirement. Naomi is another former paper worker in her fifties who desires full-time work. She is a highly skilled worker, with multiple certifications as an industrial electrician, all of which she achieved during thirty-five years of employment at the paper mill. She is married to another former paper worker who also lost his job when the plant closed. A medical condition limits Naomi's employment possibilities, but she prefers not to do menial labor or to receive disability compensation. Naomi hopes to work in her chosen field as an electrician in an industrial setting. A paper worker who worked fifty-three years in the mill, Rose is a single woman who had the additional responsibility of caring for her sisters and parents for many years. Currently she is retired and in her seventies. Stella, Rose's long-time co-worker, is a happily retired single woman in her sixties who has worked part-time as a restaurant hostess since the mill closed. Stella worked in the paper mill for forty-nine years. A fifth paper worker, Suzanne, is also married to another former paper worker. In her fifties, she is enjoying her retirement from the mill. Following its closing, Suzanne has done extensive volunteer work in her community.

Two of the women in this study are African American members of the United Steel Workers of America (USWA). Both work in the tire manufacturing industry in an urban area. Their marital status is unknown to me since this fact did not emerge in their narratives, and I did not specifically inquire. Kim is a leader in the USWA district as a member of the executive board. She is a woman in her fifties who has worked in the industry for twenty-one years. She has three grown children. Millie is a woman in her forties who has worked in textiles, automobile parts assembly, and the tire industry. However, her first union job was in tire manufacturing with the USWA. She has been with her current employer since 1989. Millie also serves as a representative for her union local executive board.

Several respondents in this project work or have worked in telecommunications; all are white women. They are or have been members of the Communication Workers of America (CWA). Sally is in her fifties and, with thirty-six years in the industry, has the longest employment tenure of any of the currently employed women in this study. She is married to another CWA member, and they have one child. A former member of the CWA, Lynda is a single woman in her late forties. Currently she works in the telecommunications industry, having been employed with the same company for twenty-six years. She became disillusioned with the CWA early in her career and remains anti-union. Ellen is in her fifties and is also married to another CWA member; however, she retired after thirty-one years of working in telecommunications. During her work tenure, Ellen held many leadership positions in the CWA. Currently she works as a labor activist, advocating for workers' rights in North Carolina. Ellen also serves as a volunteer in a number of community endeavors.

SILENT AND VOICED: NARRATIVES OF WORKING-CLASS WOMEN

Feminist thinkers have examined the ways that patriarchy and the dominant male culture have oppressed women, effectively silencing them. In *The Psychic Life of Power*, Judith Butler investigates the ways that power relations affect discourse. Butler, quoting Wittgenstein, notes, "'We speak, we utter words, and only later get a sense of their life.' Anticipation of such sense governs the 'empty' ritual that is speech, and ensures its iterability."[23] Butler also refers to Hegel's bondsman whose work is conscripted. The phenomenology of his life work is consumed by others in power over him. He fears this consumption as a loss of self. As Butler explains it,

> [The] bondsman understands two issues: first, that what he is is embodied or signified in what he makes, and second, that what he makes is made under the compulsion to give it up. Hence, if the object defines him, reflects back what he is, is the signatory text by which he acquires a sense of who he is, and if those objects are relentlessly sacrificed, then he is a relentlessly self-sacrificing being. He can recognize his own signature only as what is constantly being erased, as a persistent site of vanishing.[24]

While these self-sacrificing conditions may result in a form of silence, many workers nonetheless have rich and complex private and public lives, bolstered by various sources of strength, such as their work, unions, churches, and families. The women in this study employ a variety of these strategies of self-advocacy and self-worth. While many of the women I interviewed eventually claim their power and agency, a few are indeed silenced by the external and internal influences of oppression.

Although the self-sacrifice inherent in most employment may silence workers, an academic or formal discourse of those in power may also silence them. In his discussion of oral versus print societies in *Biosphere Politics*, Jeremy Rifkin notes that oral cultures are particularly intimate and social. Learning is done in social contexts with stories and proverbs serving as the "most common forms of transferring knowledge between people and generations."[25] In opposition to this culture of intimacy and shared knowledge, the print culture "reinforces isolation over group participation. Writing and reading are activities best pursued in privacy."[26] Rifkin further states that "print detaches people from each other" and is an "artificial construct."[27] The printing press "allowed words to be privatized and commercialized for the first time in history. In an oral culture, words, stories, tales, poems, and aphorisms were all collectively shared."[28] Words, language, and stories transformed into print become property, privatized and commodified. The silences of working-class women may be a direct result of their resisting commodification by outsiders and those in power.

This objectification of their life stories may be the reason why some of the women in this study would decide—after initially agreeing to do so—that they would not participate or why they disclosed little about their personal lives. When I interviewed Millie, she told me little of her personal story. After providing information about the strike and her work at the plant, Millie barely answered my follow-up questions about her strength and determination to persist during difficult times. She said, "Actually, I think it's my mom. She's my mentor." Other than a brief comment about her mother's work as a minister, Millie returned to discussing her work with no mention of her personal experiences and the qualities that led to her success. Perhaps Millie purposely chose to limit my access to her private, personal life. Perhaps that aspect of her life is sacrosanct. Like Hegel's bondsman, Millie had labored for her company, creating products that bore no mark of her work. I may have represented yet another authority figure trying to take away and commodify a part of her life for my own uses.

While Millie and other women often claim their own power in refusing commodification, psychologist Carol Gilligan demonstrates the damaging results if women fail to do so. In her seminal feminist work, *In a Different Voice*, Gilligan explores the suffocating effects of women's failure to claim their voices. Their silence is indicative of their submission to a patriarchal code that has effectively trivialized or marginalized the voices of women. Her studies led Gilligan to note that women's psychological development in a patriarchal society leads them to censor themselves and to devalue their experiences. In Gilligan's view, silence can only be pathological, damaging to all women.

Choices not to speak are often well-intentioned and psychologically protective, motivated by concerns for people's feelings and by an awareness of the realities of one's own and others' lives. And yet by restricting their voices, many women are wittingly or unwittingly perpetuating a male-voiced civilization and an order of living that is founded on disconnection from women.[29]

Adding women's voices to those of men, Gilligan notes, "literally changes the voice: how the human story is told, and also who tells it."[30] She later notes that to "have a voice is to be human. To have something to say is to be a person. But speaking depends on listening and being heard; it is an intensely relational act."[31]

However, in their unequal relations, women's voices are often suppressed, even though as Gilligan notes, speaking and "listening are a form of psychic breathing."[32] The lack of psychological space often leaves women feeling powerless. Even if women wanted to fight these forces, without "voice, there is no possibility for resistance."[33] Women ultimately dissociate from their lived experiences, Gilligan suggests, and "men and women tacitly collude in not voicing women's experiences, building relationships around a silence that is maintained by men's not knowing their disconnection from women and women's not knowing their dissociation from themselves."[34] This dissociation leads to a loss of identity and lack of empowerment.

In this study, women often reported that they were silenced by their male relatives, colleagues, and supervisors through coercion, oppression, or physical force. For example, Lynda's narrative, recounted over nine hours in three separate interviews, relates a series of events that deny her right to a voice and self-advocacy beginning at a young age. When she was eleven years old, Lynda ran away from her overbearing father. She describes the scene when her father caught her.

He took each article out of the suitcase outside, made me stand in the snow and ice, and he said, "I bought this, I paid for this, so I'm throwing it away. Let me tell you something. When you leave this house, you will take with you only what you own and nothing else. And you will work for what you get." Boy, that made an impression on me like nothing you would believe. I was terrified. And I never forgot that.

As a result, Lynda went to work at age fifteen in order to begin the process of claiming herself. In the meantime, she grew up in an oppressive environment. She later states, "Growing up was like prison. Dad was real controlling. I wasn't allowed to date. He was real strict. So when I left, [he told me]: 'I own you until you're eighteen; I own you until you're eighteen.'" Not only is Lynda not heard, she is also not acknowledged as a separate being of her own. Lynda began to find her voice when she left home to attend college; however, she eventually dropped out and, as she put it, "disappeared," yet another form of silence.

SILENCE AND POWER RELATIONS

Complementing Gilligan's research, Mary Belenky and her colleagues at Harvard explored the ways that women negotiated power relations in their higher education experiences. In their study, *Women's Ways of Knowing*, these researchers found that the "male experience has been so powerfully articulated that we believed we would hear the patterns in women's voices more clearly if we held at bay the powerful templates men have etched in the literature and in our minds."[35] Silence, for Belenky and others, is an epistemological position whereby "women experience themselves as mindless and voiceless and subject to the whims of external authority."[36] This position is the lowest level of knowing, a self-abnegating activity for women. In addition, the researchers found that even when women are able to speak and to assert themselves, their voices are often unheard or devalued. "Some women told us, in anger and frustration, how frequently they felt unheard and unheeded—both at home and at work. . . . Once a woman has a voice, she wants it to be heard."[37] Indeed whenever women find their voices, too often their perspectives or their experiences are denigrated or ignored, resulting in a silence that berefts the work world in particular, whenever "their 'womanly voice' was dismissed as soft or misguided, a particularly common complaint of women working in a setting where men predominated."[38] One professional woman in the study commented that she would talk about things she cared about only if she felt that the other person was "really listening. If I don't feel that, I find myself falling into a silence . . . ."[39]

For women in this study, these silences, both imposed and self-directed, limit their experiences and power in the work place. For Ellen, a retired telecommunications worker, male colleagues and supervisors effectively stifled her contributions for many years, especially early in her career when she was one of only a few women in the entire state to work in the utilities industry. She related her experiences with one particular supervisor who, as she said, "hated women." He kept her isolated and overworked while maintaining a hostile environment. When Ellen told her supervisor that he was being unfair and that she would not do work that was not her responsibility, he "wrote [her] up for insubordination." She filed a grievance. At her hearing, both the union president and the supervisor effectively silenced Ellen with their arguments and verbal abuse. She thought, "I'm fired. I am just absolutely fired." While she won her case and eventually left that job, Ellen was not allowed to represent herself at the meeting. In a separate instance, Ellen was elected as a political liaison for the mountain district in which she worked. Though this role should have given Ellen the right to use her voice, she said that she was told how to vote and that her own voice must remain silent. "Women were told what position they were going to take on certain issues. And before I left town I knew how I was supposed to vote because it had kind of been given to me." Ellen's experiences indicate how the workplace and the union, both dominated by men, oppress and silence women.

For Ellen and many other women involved in unions in the twentieth century, their silences are indicative of oppression and loss. In *Silences,* Tillie Olsen speaks of these "unnatural" silences, noting that women writers were effectively silenced by not being published or by being forgotten after an initial success. "These are not natural silences, that necessary time for renewal, lying fallow, gestation, in the natural cycle of creation. The silences I speak of here are unnatural; the unnatural thwarting of what struggles to come into being, but cannot."[40] In like fashion, many of the women in this study come late to finding their voices and adding their ideas to those of men in the workplace and in the union, or else they become completely passive and fail to find their voices. These institutions are diminished by the lack of women's engagement with their minds and hearts to the business at hand. Olsen says that the most mournful silences are those "where the lives never came to writing. Among these, the mute inglorious Miltons: those whose waking hours are all struggle for existence; the barely educated; the illiterate; women. Their silence the silence of centuries as to how life was, is, for most of humanity."[41] Likewise, union leadership and work organizations reflect these silences. In her litany of loss, Olsen lists the varieties of silence: censorship, politics, perfectionism, marginalism, "sacrifice of talent, in pieces to preserve its essential value," absences, premature silences, foreground silences, and "silences where the lives never come to writing."[42] The working women's lives that never come to *speaking and acting* also leave the world bereft.

When Annie, one of the women in this study, is silenced, an entire community loses its collective voice for workplace democracy. As a "scab," or replacement worker, at the age of fifteen during the General Textile Strike of 1934, Annie later learns about the power of a union while working at a unionized munitions plant during World War II. As a shop steward, Annie took the women workers' concerns about pay inequities to the union, which led to changes that equalized all workers' pay. When the war ended, Annie returned to work at the textile plant in her small hometown, newly aware that mill workers were being treated unfairly. She attempted to organize a union in 1950, an undertaking that failed, causing her great personal and financial losses. After she began her organizing campaign, Annie was fired on the first day that she missed work to tend her sick child. Though she filed a National Labor Relations Board suit against the company, the litigation took six years, and she was "blackballed," or blacklisted, at every company in the county as a "troublemaker." She was unable to find work in the county.

Annie's voice was effectively silenced, as was the union and the collective power of workers in her community, when the company instituted its union-busting tactics. However, these strategies hurt a well-meaning woman in ways that still affect her life, though she is now in her eighties. Karmen MacKendrick speaks of this type of silencing. "It is the speaking 'I,' the I who can say, 'I want, I will, I know' as much as 'I am,' who must fall silent, who must know nothing, who must, in forgetting, exceed every *must* in moving beyond and before any memory of itself."[43] Annie was forced into this untenable position. Her brother worked as a manager in the mill and daily attempted to coerce her into dropping the lawsuit. She says that he relentlessly pursued this course.

> At about one o'clock, [my brother] came to my home and said, "I hate you got messed up in this union business. Why don't you get out and get on the winning side? If the election had been held about a month ago, they might have won, but not now. I think I have enough influence with [the superintendent] to get you back to work if you will go back and withdraw from the union and drop your charges against the company." See, that's [my brother] trying to get me to drop the charges.

Annie also recounted the ways that the company officials tried to get her to drop the suit. One supervisor told her, "We have our warehouses full of cloth. [Unionization] is one thing that our company cannot [allow]. As long as [the workers] are going to [make] strike trouble, this will hurt the people and not me. *You will be the one hurt if there is labor trouble*" (her emphasis). These threats, combined with the loss of her job, effectively silenced both Annie and the union voice in her community. The employees at the mill—the largest employer in the town—never successfully organized or joined a union.

SILENCE AS A FORM OF FEMINIST POWER

While many feminist philosophers and social scientists have explored women's silence as a negative consequence of oppression and the patriarchal strictures placed on women in unequal power relations, other thinkers have posed opposite ideas. If, like Hegel's bondsman, women have felt that they own their words and that others may not conscript their "property," then perhaps they also resist any attempt to essentialize both their experiences and their identities. The production of storytelling that results in a final solid identity is resisted in the silences of people who want to retain the ownership of their identities. In *The Silent Cry: Mysticism and Resistance*, Dorothee Soelle echoes the idea that speech itself becomes a commodity, stating that we "ensilence the experience, and it is a star that travels along its path. We speak it, and it is thrown down under the treads of the market."[44] Women resist commodification of their identity, for as Hannah Arendt notes in *The Human Condition*, the "unchangeable identity of the person, though disclosing itself intangibly in act and speech, becomes tangible only in the story of the actor's and speaker's life; but as such it can be known . . . only after it has come to an end."[45] In other words, only after a person dies can those who survive ascribe a final identity through his or her life story. In some instances the women I interviewed were silent about certain aspects of their lives, maintaining their power to determine their own lives and their own identities.

Throughout our interview, one woman in this project, Joan, maintained distance from her personal life during her narrative. During the strike at her plant, Joan was a union leader who became a spokesperson for the striking workers and thus became a target, which literally endangered her life on several occasions. As a leader, Joan was often called upon to represent the workers' and the union's views for the media. She stated that she had been misquoted so often by members of the press that she was leery of being interviewed. Joan insisted on seeing anything I wrote about her before it was printed. Of the respondents, she was also the most interested in the study guidelines and release form, reading the paperwork carefully and making several comments about withdrawing from the study whenever she wished. During our short interview, Joan related incidents from the difficulties that she and her fellow workers faced when they were engaged in the strike, including misrepresentation in the press. "Of course the news media was always there. They . . . never report the true story."

As the leader of the striking workers, Joan was often attacked. "I was so bitter because the company . . . turned everything on *me*" (her emphasis). When the strike was over, matters did not improve for Joan. She states that the company "did everything they could to make my life miserable." Following her narrative about the strike, I asked Joan a personal question. I wanted to know the sources of her strength and determination. She replied that when her father left the family, as the oldest of six children, she had to be responsible and help take care of her siblings. "My mother depended on me for *everything*." However, she does not offer any other details, finally noting that "I'm not gonna let anybody just . . . take *advantage* of me." When I asked for the names of other women who were on strike with her so that I could interview them, Joan said, "No, I won't give you their names." She did agree to give my information to the other women who had been on strike though to date no one has contacted me.

Joan's silence is a tribute to her strength of purpose and sense of self. She is protecting not only herself but also her compatriots in the union. Carol Gilligan states that "you cannot take a life out of history, that life-history and history, psychology, and politics, are deeply intertwined."[46] Susan Sontag, in "The Aesthetics of Silence," offers a possible different interpretation of the women's silences in this study, including Joan's. Sontag suggests that language is "weighed down by historical accumulation."[47] Therefore the speaker is dealing with "two potentially antagonistic domains of meaning and their relationships. One is his own meaning (or lack of it); the other is the set of second-order meanings that both extend his own language and encumber, compromise, and adulterate it."[48] Joan's experience with the printed word and with people in power led to her decisions to protect herself from what she saw as inappropriate prying in order to appropriate her personal narrative. According to Jill Taylor and others, in *Voice and Silence: Women, Girls, Race, and Relationship*, women "can maintain a public silence or remain outspoken; either way, if they feel that 'no one listens' or that 'you can't trust anybody,' they are likely to find that they are disconnected from themselves and from others and 'not really tell anybody anything.'"[49] Joan's silences are indicative of her lack of trust in those who represent her words.

THE TRANSCENDENCE OF NARRATIVE

While I may be perceived as an outsider in the working-class culture by the women I interviewed, as a daughter of that culture, I do not feel the distance from these workers in the same ways as they do. However, I must admit that I no longer "fit" in this world because of my current work and movement to the middle class. Therefore, now I am really outside of their experience even though I have worked in a factory and held other working-class jobs. As an outsider, I have conflicts in presenting or re-presenting the voice of the

"Other," as Gayatri Spivak suggests in "Can the Subaltern Speak?" Spivak, contrary to Foucault and Deleuze, challenges the idea that the oppressed can "speak, act, and know *for themselves.*"[50] Rather than a reductionist, formalist theory of the Other as a single entity, Spivak insists that in the "'true' subaltern group, whose identity is its difference, there is no unrepresentable subaltern subject that can know and speak itself."[51] Furthermore, in considering the voices of women, Spivak argues that rather than representing a unified viewpoint, "the most that one can sense is the immense heterogeneity breaking through . . . ."[52] To do otherwise is to participate in the "ideological epistemic violence" that minimizes women's voices.

From a different perspective, in *Fruits of Sorrow*, Elizabeth Spelman argues that giving voice to the "subaltern" is necessary since the oppressed person must be taken seriously. She notes that

> Harriet Jacobs clearly wanted her voice as a female slave to be heard for several reasons: to provide an accurate view of what slavery entailed; to establish her presence as someone who had not been and would not be reduced to the status of a passive voiceless victim; and to ensure that the focus of the suffering of slavery includes those who are responsible for it, not just those who endure its horrors.[53]

The women who freely share the painful aspects of their lives make it possible for other women to relate their experiences, not as "passive voiceless victims" but as actors in their own struggles to be heard. Women's stories of survival and transcendence empower other women to resist oppression and to find their voices. As Clarissa Pinkola Estes states in *The Gift of Story*,

> It must be noted also that many of the most powerful medicines, that is stories, come about as a result of one person's or group's terrible and compelling suffering. For the truth is that much of story comes from travail; theirs, ours, mine, yours, someone's we know, someone's we do not know far away in time and place. And yet, paradoxically, these very stories that rise from deep suffering can provide the most potent remedies for past, present, and even future ills.[54]

Estes believes in the healing power of stories and therefore resists what Olsen calls "unnatural" silences. "Though none of us will live forever, the stories can. As long as one soul remains who can tell the story, and that by the recounting of the tale, the greater forces of love, mercy, generosity and strength are continuously called into being in the world."[55] Storytelling provides the means for empowerment and transcendence.

Indeed, as Audre Lorde notes in her essay, "Age, Race, Class, and Sex: Women Redefining Difference," the "future of the earth may depend upon the ability of all women to identify and develop new definitions of power and new patterns of relating across difference."[56] Invoking Paolo Friere, Lorde states that "the true focus of revolutionary change is never merely the oppressive situations which we seek to escape, but that piece of the oppressor which is planted deep within each of us, and which knows only the oppressors' tactics, the oppressors' relationships."[57] Whether to transcend the oppressive nature of silences compelled by patriarchy and other power relations or to claim their self-chosen silences and voices, women must recognize that they have the right to either.

ORGANIZING THE NARRATIVE STUDY

In this chapter I introduced the rationale for this project, giving voice to work-ing-class women while respecting their self-imposed silences. Chapter two outlines the research methodology in its theoretical and political frameworks. The analysis of the women's narratives in this study utilizes a protocol devel-oped by Carolyn Riessman, and depends theoretically and politically on the working-class narratology of Alessandro Portelli and the feminist psychol-ogy of Carol Gilligan. In chapter two, I also discuss the process of planning the project, identifying and contacting the respondents, conducting the inter-views, and completing the analyses. Finally, I locate the thematic sources of the women's narratives into four coherent discourse communities and present possible interpretations of their stories.

In chapter three, I introduce a discourse community based on women's self-identities developed through their work in male-dominated fields. In non-traditional roles, these women have exhibited strength and determination to succeed despite multiple challenges. Chapter four focuses on the lives of women unionists who identify strongly with their role as activists for their sisters and brothers in the union. These women have endeavored to improve the lives of others by working for empowerment and equity for all workers. In chapter five, I explore the narratives of women who have sacrificed much in their personal and work lives and identify with a martyr role, whether in their families and communities or in their unions and companies. Chapter six highlights the lives of the new union feminists, those women who have the confidence and leadership skills to transform their own and others' lives, effectively transcending patriarchy and class oppression. They all are empow-ered by their exuberant independence and keen willingness to fight discrimi-nation and injustice, qualities that inevitably benefit other women and men in the workplace.

Chapter Two
A Feminist Working-Class Narrative Study

This study employs a research methodology that depends on narrative analysis and interpretation. This is essentially a feminist approach since narratology explores subjectivity, connectivity, and identity, giving agency to respondents who are constructing meaning within their own social, historical, and cultural contexts. Using a five-step model proposed by Catherine Riessman in *Narrative Analysis*, this study involves attending (to respondents), telling (to the researcher), transcribing, analyzing, and reading (of the final text.) The sole prompt for respondents was "I am interested in women who have been involved in strikes. Tell me the story of your life." This query gave respondents many possible choices in narrative structure and meanings. Focusing on the resulting narrative texts, I discovered commonalities and coherence across events and themes as constructed through the respondents' use of language and metaphors.

MYSELF AS A RESEARCHER

I situate myself as a working-class daughter of the textile industry and have inevitably interpreted these women's narratives through the lens of my own experiences. My background intersects in various ways with the lives of the working-class women I interviewed. I first became interested in the stories of women involved in labor disputes as I developed the initial strands of research about women who worked in textile mills. I grew up in a textile mill town, and both of my grandfathers, one grandmother, my father, my mother, and most of my aunts and uncles worked at the mill. One day, while talking with my mother about the topic, I asked a seemingly random question, "Did anyone ever try to organize a union at the mill?" She said that "Annie" had attempted to organize the mill and that she might still be alive. This idea interested me, and I wrote to Annie, explaining that I would like to talk to her about her experiences. In my letter I indicated that she likely remembered my grandparents and my father from the mill. About a week later Annie called my grandmother to confirm the information that I had sent. I then contacted Annie and arranged for an interview. Annie shared the remarkable story of her six-year dispute with the mill for illegally firing her because she tried to organize a union. Thus Annie's account helped focus my research on the stories of women involved in labor disputes.

As a researcher, I am inevitably influenced by my working-class background. My father, a high school dropout, is a retired brick mason, and my mother, who attended college only after she was forty years old, is a retired teacher. None of my grandparents finished high school, and all but one worked in the cotton mill in our town. In fact, one grandfather died soon after his retirement from the mill, and the other grandfather gradually went deaf after working for years in the "weave room." He worked at the mill for fifty-one years, beginning when he was orphaned at age eleven. With this history, the cotton mill is an abiding backdrop to our family's stories, a continuing influence in our family's thinking, and an ever-present symbol of our past entanglements with factory and "mill hill," or mill village, life. In fact, my father's autonomy in his trade as a brick mason came after years of working at the mill, yearning for the outdoors he so loved. Meanwhile my mother was constantly reading and learning, pining for a college education, a dream that she finally realized at the age of forty-four. While immediate and extended family members enjoy the freedom and autonomy that the changing economy and suburban lifestyle are bringing to our hometown, most of them are nostalgic for the close-knit mill community that we once knew. The town is changing rapidly, and we are often reminded of the disappearing relics of that long-gone community, such as when a large section of the abandoned mill was razed in 2003 to create a new business.

As a researcher, I am also shaped by my own work conflicts with college administrators during the past fifteen years. Often my supervisors and I have disagreed on issues relating to faculty workload, salary inequities, class size, and adjunct instructors' pay, among other issues. While I value cooperation, I also advocate for equality, justice, and democracy in the workplace. In addition, my experiences as an organizer for Beyond War, a grassroots peace organization, and as a member of the North Carolina Community College Faculty Association also shaped my interest in the solidarity and economic welfare of workers. Currently, I am a member of the State Employees Association of North Carolina, which is affiliated with the Service Employees International Union (SEIU). I also support the HOPE Coalition (Hear Our Public Employees), formed to raise awareness and work toward repeal of North Carolina Statutes 95–98, which bar state employees from the collective bargaining process.

IDENTIFYING THE RESPONDENTS

After I focused the study on collecting and analyzing the narratives of women who have been involved in labor disputes, I investigated ways of identifying potential respondents. Because there are few companies with union members in the state and even fewer women unionists, I knew that it would be difficult to find women who fit the criteria and who would be willing to participate. On two occasions, I conducted research in the North Carolina Collection and the Southern Historical Collection at the University of North Carolina at Chapel Hill. I reviewed texts and newspaper articles about the various strikes that have occurred in the state, and I made a list of the strikes and the counties in which they occurred. I then contacted local history reference librarians in those communities to find contact persons who could direct me to women who are veterans of strikes. In addition, James Andrews, president of the North Carolina AFL-CIO, graciously provided contact information for several of the women that I interviewed. These women in turn were helpful in directing me to their colleagues who had been involved in strikes.

In some cases, I contacted people I know who live in these communities, and I asked if they knew any women who had been involved in strikes. Whenever I made contact with a potential respondent this way, I asked if the woman would give me names and telephone numbers of other women who were on strike with her. On at least one occasion, this tactic led to interviews with four additional women. However, this method had one drawback: the women were aware that other people in the community knew that they were participating when I had promised them anonymity. At other times, I contacted individuals who had been interviewed by other researchers, as in the 1958 Harriet-Henderson strike when I contacted one woman from that dispute after finding her name in the telephone directory. I also asked a friend in the Communication Workers of America if he could recommend any women unionists who would have been employed in 1984, the year of the last strike. These leads provided me with the names of nearly 20 women from all areas in North Carolina except the southeastern region of the state. When I contacted the southeastern Central Labor Council official, she told me that most of the union members in that part of the state are federal employees and therefore have not participated in strikes. Without fail, all of the people I asked were eager to help me, and I am grateful for their assistance.

Several of the women I contacted did not want to be interviewed, and I attribute this to wanting to forget the painful incidents of the past, to a lack of trust in me and my purposes, and to fear of others knowing that they talked about their strike experiences. In some cases, the women live in communities where people want to forget that the labor disputes even happened, as in Henderson where archives about the Harriet-Henderson strike are repeatedly stolen from the public library. On one occasion, a respondent declined to participate after initially being enthusiastic and directing me to nearly a dozen other women in her community. When I arrived in her community and contacted her to confirm our appointment, she became hostile and asked why I was talking only with women. She also wanted to know why I had contacted her and not the local union office. One of her colleagues, a woman who had to ask her husband's permission to be interviewed, later told me that she couldn't participate. Previously she had been eager to talk with me since she had lost her job with only six months remaining until her retirement. She also informed me that she had been out on strike for nearly a year, but that her husband had crossed the picket line. When I talked to her by telephone, she stated, "I'm sorry, but I can't do it. I'm a preacher's wife. I can't get involved." My research likely would have taken different paths if these women had participated.

When I contacted the women who participated, I informed them that I was a graduate student collecting the stories of women in North Carolina who had been on strike. I also told them that if they chose to tell their stories, I would protect their anonymity. Of the women who elected to participate in the project, I collected thirteen useable narratives. The ten white and three African American respondents are or were members of six different unions in four different industries based in eight cities and towns across the state. The ages of the women range from mid-forties to late eighties. Five of the women are currently working; five are retired; and three are unemployed but seeking employment.

In this study, I refer to each of the respondents by pseudonyms in order to maintain confidentiality and to protect their anonymity, a condition of this research. Joan, Katherine, and Annie are former textile employees, and Ellen, Lynda, and Sally are current and former telecommunications workers. Suzanne, Rose, Camille, Stella, and Naomi are all former paper workers, and Kim and Millie are currently employed in the tire manufacturing industry. Each of these women has contributed to my understanding of work in companies with union representation and their participation in labor disputes; in addition, each woman offered her perspective in a spirit of improving the conditions of labor for all working-class women and men.

EMOTIONS AND FIELDWORK: COLLECTING NARRATIVES

Much of this research was shaped by the theory and practice of Sherryl Kleinman and Martha A. Copp in *Emotions and Fieldwork*, in which qualitative research methods incorporate the researcher's reactions, responses, and emotions as essential components of the research process. These authors suggest that qualitative researchers should forgo attempts to legitimize the methodology of qualitative inquiry. Rather, social scientists who employ qualitative methods should embrace the seeming subjectivities and real emotionalities that often form the crux of these modes and either overtly or intuitively lead researchers to valuable, unforeseen insights.

A lack of awareness of the essential, foundational nature of emotions in fieldwork often results in researchers' emotional reactions being more difficult impediments to the work than a full acceptance of and reliance on expressed and interpreted feelings would have been. Relying on their innate sensibilities and trusting their intuitive responses led Kleinman and Copp and many of their fellow researchers to develop specific methods to utilize this "symbolic interactionist perspective" into their work.[1] Kleinman explains: "What I came to realize much later was that these critiques of the setting (and study) were also *data*. Our negative reactions reflected the society in which the Center was located and with which it had to struggle, a society where assumptions about legitimacy run deep."[2] In response to the propensity of qualitative researchers to become external apologists, if not internal self-doubters, these authors call on scholars who employ this methodology to question the positivist position and to embrace the holistic, responsive, social construction of emotion that informs and enhances research. "'Qualitative researchers only gain control of their projects by first allowing themselves to lose it.'"[3] Losing control, as Kleinman and Copp put it, enabled me to tap into an intuitive understanding of this project, of the individuals interviewed, and of myself as a researcher, for it is indeed *how* one studies as much as *what* one investigates that matters in qualitative research. In fact, as these authors point out, researchers who conduct field work are inextricably linked to their subjects in ways they may not fully realize.

> [H]aving a professional identity allows us to ignore that we enact a variety of social identities in the field . . . . Fieldworkers enter the field as more than researchers. Our identities and life experiences shape the political and ideological stances we take in our research. As Elizabeth Fee (1988) put it, "The idea of a pure knowing mind

outside history is simply an epistemological conceit." . . . Ignoring
the interplay of person and research ultimately has analytic costs.[4]

Kleinman's example of research in a seminary demonstrates this idea
since her deeply rooted white liberal identity prevented a full study
because of the ways that she excluded the black seminary students. "My
white liberal ideology, then, kept me from gathering data (or examining
the data that I had) that might portray the black students as less than
perfect humanitarians. Was I only trying to protect the black students?
No. I also protected my liberal self-image."[5] Her self-protection became
a major impediment to a full study.

As researchers, our emotions and identities are tightly bound to our
subjects and projects and profoundly influence what as well as how we
study. Field workers therefore must have a means of bringing their emotions into the foreground. It is crucial for analytic integrity. As Kleinman
states: "We must consider who we are and what we believe when we do
fieldwork. Otherwise we might not see how we shape the story. Perhaps
later, once we are involved in our next project, we will recognize gaps in
our earlier analyses that resulted from our tightly held views. We do ourselves a favor if we reflect on these matters while we are in the field."[6]
Moreover, qualitative researchers should engage in thorough examina-
tions of their emotional responses, both positive and negative, ultimately
striving for understanding and clarity.

The success of a research project depends as much on the objective
accounts of this "data" as it does on the other aspects of fieldwork. In
constructing objective written accounts, Kleinman and Copp caution that
both sympathetic and unsympathetic responses need to be examined and
interpreted fully. "[U]nlike other professionals whose goal is detached
concern . . . fieldworkers expect to have powerful feelings. But we
place conditions on ourselves. First, we want to have only strongly positive feelings. Second, we want to have them within an appropriate relationship, namely friendship."[7] Using feelings as "clues," researchers may
discover new insights unattainable through a distanced "objectivity."

> We can learn from any vantage point as long as we know what roles
> we occupy in different situations. Our feelings while in a particular role
> might mirror those who hold a similar role in the setting. . . . Thus our
> feelings suggest hypotheses about how others, members of a subgroup in
> the setting or perhaps outsiders, feel about themselves and each other. If
> we examine our uncomfortable feelings rather than dismiss them, we can
> gain insights into how others feel and why.[8]

This approach allowed me to empathize with my respondents without concern that I was not being objective or sufficiently analytical. Rather, I was able to bond with these women, and in some cases, to develop ongoing friendships. A connected perspective that incorporates emotions made my research even more meaningful in unforeseen ways.

INTERVIEWS AND ANALYSIS

When I had completed the interviews, I analyzed and interpreted the narrative texts, exploring the selectivities, slippages, and silences to determine whether there are intertexualities in the lived experiences of North Carolina women who actively participated in the historical, political, and personal act of engaging in strikes. Selectivities in each narrative are the respondent's choices of topics, language, and metaphors. Slippages are instances where the respondent's narrative reveals inconsistent information, such as dates or events, and silences are the omissions from each respondent's narrative, areas of her life that are not included in her story. My research philosophy and practice mirrors that of historian Lu Ann Jones in *Mama Learned Us to Work: Farm Women in the New South*. She describes her intentions as follows:

> As I saw it, my task as an interviewer was to help people describe . . . broad economic and social change in personal terms and to interpret the interplay between structural changes and family and community life. Because I wanted to share interpretive authority with narrators, I was ready for them to challenge and complicate the received scholarly wisdom. I also began the fieldwork determined to listen to women as well as to men.[9]

As Jones has done, in conducting this research, I hoped to create a space where these women's voices will be heard in the ongoing labor struggles in the state, the nation, and the world so that they might speak *to* those in power and *for* those who have yet to claim power.

THEORY AND METHODOLOGY

The interpretive community shared by all of the respondents is one of working-class women in the South. The language of self-reliance and independence, the metaphors of church and family, and the ideals of pride in one's work and proving oneself worthy all characterize the collective-subjective of working-class women in the twentieth-century South. While each of these women speaks to the power relations inherent in her work life, all respond in varying ways, according to the dictates of the self, identities constructed by their stories. As Kathleen Casey points out in *I Answer with My Life: Life Histories of Women Teachers Working for Social Change*: "[E]very study of narrative is based on a particular understanding of the speaker's self."[10] Therefore each of the women frames her experiences in particular ways while retaining "authority" as an expert of her own life story.

My methodology echoes that of Kathleen Casey, who asks readers to consider the cacophonous din of powerful conservative voices responding to perceived "crises" in American education. She points out the agendas (hidden and open) of the forces and factions bearing down on education, teachers, and students. Casey directs the reader to listen to the often unheard, yet insightful, voices of students and teachers. My own project reflects a similar aim of providing a means for working women to find their voices—to make meaning and to create history. Further, their storytelling is a way of empowering themselves and others. Because I seek to empower the women I interviewed—extending to include all women workers—I have endeavored to make their lives visible on the printed page. Each of the women, as part of an interpretive community, adopts similar perspectives and patterns of priorities that cohere into insights about the working lives of North Carolina women during this time. In analyzing the respondents' narratives, four distinct intertextualities, or connected links, emerge among their topics, language, and metaphors.

As I will show in subsequent chapters, these connections result in distinct discourse or collective-subjective interpretive communities, including four women who identified with their work in "men's" jobs; three women who serve as union activists; three women who become martyrs for their families and unions; and three women who adopt a union feminist approach to their lives and work. However, I realize that these women's experiences are limited by language and interpretation, for as Chris Weedon points out in *Feminist Practice and Poststructuralist Theory*, language "offers a range of ways of interpreting our lives which imply different versions of experience."[11] Despite unavoidable misinterpretations, I hope to present these women's language and their intended meanings as much as possible.

SOCIAL AND HISTORICAL RESEARCH

The majority of research involving strikes in North Carolina includes journalists' accounts, oral histories, memoirs, fictional accounts, and traditional histories. Of the eight strikes presented in my research, the General

Textile Strike of 1934 and the Loray Mill Strike of 1929 have generated the most attention and investigation. Historical fiction has also recorded these landmarks in the labor history of the South, as I will show in chapter five. Of the volumes and articles that I read on these subjects, none shares the voices of women using a narrative research methodology. The closest kin to my study may be Victoria Byerly's *Hard Times Cotton Mill Girls*, an oral history collection of southern women who worked in textile mills. Byerly provides more traditional oral histories, presenting the words of the women in story form with no formal analysis other than organizing the narratives according to topics related to the history of textiles in the South. She states, "I began collecting data on southern textile workers with the idea that I might go back South and try my hand at oral history."[12] Byerly further explains her purpose, a deeply personal one:

> When I returned, after talking to hundreds of mill workers, I began to reconstruct a feeling of belonging that I had felt only as a small child, and I began to see the struggles of these people in a very different light. I realized that I had never been really poor. In fact, those mill workers whom I had known as a child seemed to be reaping the modest rewards of their lifetime struggles: they had homes—some quite cozy—indoor plumbing, and food to eat. The streets had been paved and children now played softball with real bats instead of sticks.[13]

From my perspective, Byerly's research is nostalgic, romanticizing the experiences of the women that she interviewed. Had she attempted to study their language and metaphors, Byerly likely would have written a different book. She acknowledges the forces that have kept working women in poverty. "Mill women continue to come up against oppression on a daily basis. Southern mill women's strength lies not so much in their ability to organize successfully to counter the tactics of the powerful textile industry, but in their ability to survive poverty, humiliation, and isolation from the rest of the world."[14] Nonetheless Byerly ignores the solidarity of women who participated in strikes and who want to do more than just survive.

In *Civil Rights Unionism: Tobacco Workers and the Struggle for Democracy in the Mid-Twentieth-Century South*, labor historian Robert Korstad provides a framework for incorporating the voices of women and men in his study of the tobacco industry in Winston-Salem, North Carolina in the 1940s. He interviewed more than a hundred people during his research and situated his study in the context of the workers' narratives. Therefore his text interweaves the oral histories of the people who lived through the events as well as the social-historical framework of economic, racial, and cultural conditions. Korstad notes: "Winston-Salem was not only a city of blue-collar workers, it was a city of *women* workers."[15] He also highlights the structures of racial capitalism, the political and racial oppression by white supremacist capitalists who controlled the city. However, the civil rights unionism—supported in large measure by women unionists—that emerged was based on solidarity with all workers—black and white. "They believed in the long run only an interracial labor movement could achieve their broader goals."[16] With a social justice agenda of achieving civil rights and labor rights for all workers, the unionists hoped to ignite reform in the South. However, as Korstad explains, the forces of the Cold War ideology quashed the seven-year struggle for equality and improved labor conditions.

> At century's end, the South and the nation have yet to erase the color line, have yet to extend democratic citizenship to the workplace, have yet to attend to the basic health, education, and welfare needs of vulnerable citizens, have yet to create a truly participatory political system. Despite the enormous changes of the past fifty years, to which the black freedom struggle contributed mightily, the persistence of the past is everywhere apparent. Perhaps only when another generation of activists refashions the dreams of the 1940s to fit the contours of the new century will the legacy of racial capitalism be laid to rest.[17]

Korstad's model of history employs the voices of the women and men who fought in the bitter labor disputes in the tobacco industry. This method gives agency to his respondents and informs our understanding of the history of these events.

Three other researchers who use similar methods to construct social meanings in labor history have influenced this study. Leon Fink, in his study of migrant workers, *The Maya of Morganton: Work and Community in the Nuevo New South*, relies on the oral histories of workers to discuss the complexities of the poultry industry in North Carolina. Fink describes his interview method:

> Once we had established the respondent's basic connection to the story's main events, we tried to elicit a thread of life history, dipping back in time to understand the rudiments of family background, education, migration, and prior work experience. Then we zeroed in as much as possible on the migration, labor, and political experience (where applicable) in Morganton and across borders.[18]

Likewise Sherry Linkon and John Russo in their labor history study, *Steeltown U.S.A.: Work and Memory in Youngstown*, place the oral histories and memories of workers and community members as the centerpiece of their work. They situate the contexts of geography, culture, labor, and economics as the framework for interpreting the struggle to remember what most long to forget—the rise and fall of an industrial town. "What we see in the past provides a 'context of meaning' that helps people link their personal hopes with the goals of the community and thus to understand individual efforts as 'contributions to a common good.'"[19] Further, Linkon and Russo assert that forgetting the painful past leads to great losses for people and communities.

> Many see the need to end the "mill mentality" and "get over" the past as preconditions for shaping Youngstown's economic future, but this attitude is, in part, a failure of memory. In rushing to erase the difficult parts of Youngstown's history, too many people have also forgotten the powerful events that made Youngstown so important in American industrial and working-class history. Most important of these events were the fights for economic and social justice that led to an increasing standard of living for working people and the struggle to save the mills, which led to improved legislation for workers and their communities throughout the nation.[20]

Preserving memories is also important to Michael Honey who authored *Black Workers Remember: An Oral History of Segregation, Unionism, and the Freedom Struggle*, published in 2000. Honey collected the narratives of African American workers in Memphis in order to share their voices and their accounts of history witnessed first-hand. Their collective memory contributes to the greater story of conditions and struggles during a volatile time in our nation's history. Honey states that oral history "provided the only available method for uncovering an active black working class in factories and other workplaces."[21] The past does indeed inform the present, and these narratives offer insights into the lived experiences of working-class men and women so that we may more intelligently understand their lives and use this knowledge to build a better future.

> These stories ask us to rethink the origins and implications of the civil rights movement, and compel us to look once again at how barriers of race, class, and gender have shaped and continue to shape the American experience. They ask us to think about what it means to be poor,

black, and working class, and to recognize the unfinished character of
the struggle for racial and economic justice in our own time.[22]

The work of these labor historians—Fink, Linkon and Russo, and Honey—
provided me with models of effective narrative collection and utilization in
social and historical contexts.

Two other parallel studies of women and work in scholarly, "expert"
histories of working women's lives do not include the voices of the individuals they study. In Dorothy Sue Cobble's *Dishing It Out: Waitresses and Their
Unions in the Twentieth Century*, the women's voices are hidden behind the
"official" documented events in history. Cobble's purpose, she notes, is to
answer the following questions: "What would be the future of trade unionism and hence of worker power in the new postindustrialist society? Could
labor appeal to the growing female-dominated service work force, or was
it historically and irredeemably linked to the anchor of the blue-collar male
worker?"[23] While important and useful to my understanding of women in
unions and also sharing my political framework, this volume focusing on
the history of waitress unions nevertheless provided a limited perspective.
In a similar fashion, Daniel J. Clark's *Like Night and Day: Unionization in
a Southern Mill Town* offers history based on newspaper accounts, manu-
scripts, archives, and the like. Initially hopeful when I read that Clark had
interviewed some twenty-nine workers in that strike, my hopes were not
realized since he fails to offer more than paraphrased statements to support the supposed facts about the Harriet-Henderson Strike. The words,
language, and meanings of participants are absent; hence the voiceless pasts
that Cobble and Clark construct in their more positivist projects.

THE POLITICS OF WORKING-CLASS NARRATIVES

As a researcher, I count Alessandro Portelli, the Italian working-class
oral historian, as one of my theoretical forebears. In his seminal work, *The
Death of Luigi Trastulli and Other Stories: Form and Meaning in Oral
History*, Portelli locates his narrative methodology within the context of
achieving equality between the parties in his research. He notes that "there
are always two subjects to a field situation, and that the roles of 'observed'
and 'observer' are more fluid than it might appear at first glance."[24] When
interviewing working-class respondents in Italy and the United States,
Portelli learned that a dialectic of hierarchy and equality continuously
was being negotiated between himself and the individuals he interviewed.
Though he endeavored to adopt a "neutral" or objective stance, he did not
succeed in collecting the participants' authentic interpretations as he had

hoped. Portelli reports that his interviewees instead "responded not to me as a person, but to a stereotype of my class, manner, and speech. I had been playing the 'objective' researcher, and was rewarded with biased data."[25] In addition, Portelli learned that each interview became what he calls "an experiment in equality" based on social conditions, not the good of the individuals involved. "The field interview, therefore, cannot create an equality that does not exist, but demands it. The interview raises in both parties an awareness of the need for more equality in order to reach a more open communication . . . . Dealing with power openly makes a field interview an experiment in equality."[26] Portelli explains this concept further:

> Only equality prepares us to accept difference in terms other than hierarchy and subordination; on the other hand, without difference there is no equality—only sameness, which is a much less worthwhile ideal. Only equality makes the interview credible, but only difference makes it relevant. Field work is meaningful as the encounter of two subjects who recognize each other as subjects, and therefore separate, and seek to build their equality upon their difference in order to work together.[27]

In this study, I tried to develop a rapport with the women I interviewed, in part to help them understand that I am not as much an outsider as they may have thought. I tried to connect with them in personal ways by noting the commonalities we shared or by relating an anecdote about gardening or sewing whenever it was appropriate. I shared my own stories of working in a plastics manufacturing plant and told them about helping my father in construction. Whenever a woman seemed amenable to further connection, I tried to reach what Portelli calls "a more open communication." As a result, I have developed ongoing relationships with two of the women, and I visit and correspond regularly with them.

Finally, this research is informed by Portelli's explanation of three levels of narrative interpretation, including the institutional (politics, government, unions) on a national and international scale; the collective (community, neighborhood, workplace) in one's town, or locality; and personal (private life, family life, life cycle of events) in one's own home.[28] Portelli notes that these "levels are never entirely separate and discrete, since they all run simultaneously and mix together in the way people think and tell their lives. They interweave, communicate and influence each other."[29] I have incorporated Portelli's theory and methodology about the shapes, forms, and meanings of the narratives in my own project, noting each woman's philosophical framework and the ways that she interprets her experiences, whether on a personal or an institutional level. For example, Katherine interprets her experiences from a personal standpoint while Millie limits her life story to that which is contained in the institutions of work and her union.

THE POLITICS OF FEMINIST PSYCHOLOGY

This project also relies extensively on feminist psychological approaches first introduced by Carol Gilligan in *A Different Voice: Psychology Theory and Women's Development,* and in the research published by her colleagues, Mary Belenky and others, in *Women's Ways of Knowing: The Development of Self, Voice, and Mind,* in which women's knowledge, understanding, and articulation emerge despite the attempts of patriarchal systems to silence them. As noted in the introduction, I also incorporate Susan Sontag's ideas about the aesthetics of silence and Ann Oakley's feminist research methodology, echoing Portelli's theories about the power relations implicit in interviews. Indeed, Oakley insists that the traditional male model of interviewing—which purports to be objective—is not effective with women. Therefore I have employed Oakley's feminist model of a nonhierarchal dynamic wherein a "metaconversation" can emerge, empowering the person interviewed and including the interviewer equally.

Likewise, in *Relating: Dialogues and Dialectics*, Leslie Baxter and Barbara Montgomery point out that the dialectics of communication in relationships also relies on the idea that "people are at once actors and objects of their own actions . . . . People function as proactive actors who make communicative choices in how to function in their social world."[30] In a similar way, Kathleen Casey also notes that new narrative research methodology relies on the postmodern idea of celebrating the agency of those being studied. As was the case with Joan in this project, Casey explains that respondents' lives are protected by their choices. The human agency of each person should be inviolable, and respondents may disclose or not disclose according to their own dictates, not the researcher's. However, at least part of each person's identity and life experience is available to the researcher—if she will listen with a sensitive ear and a caring heart. Casey further points out that storytelling "is a 'negotiation of power,'" where even relating "'a story to a friend is risky business'"[31] Therefore the silence of women in my study—whether about power relations or personal lives—is essentially a matter of trust or self-empowerment.

In "The Silent Psychology," Barbara Jensen analyzes class differences and considers attempts to bridge the gaps between people of different classes. Echoing Spivak, she emphasizes that a reductionist approach to considering the lives of working-class people as wounded victims is a limited perspective.

> [W]hat is invisible externally to those on the outside is experienced internally as a silence. We must strain to hear silences inside silences, a cacophony of silences, all the white space and ground beneath the middle- and upper-class figures that fill up the picture that society paints. Compounding the silence of societal invisibility is classism, which promises that whatever is visible of working-class life will be regarded with contempt or pity. Classism is silence.[32]

Jensen also points out that middle-class language does not convey much of the meaning shared by working-class people who rely on "the substance within the silence."[33] This silence is key to the shared experiences of the working class. "The kind of communication available to working-class people, the patterns of speech and gestures that are specifically working-class, are built on meaningful silences, on shared implicit shades of meaning. No vehicle is provided, or allowed, for universal understanding. It is an intimate language for members only."[34] Jensen further notes that this silence may be indicative either of acceptance or resignation at the harsh realities of working-class life. However, she does not "want to deny the psychological pain, which is so plentiful for people in the working class. That, too, is close to the way we are supposed to swallow our oppression and the presumption that we really do not exist."[35] She points out that "there is no denying the demoralizing effects of all these silences" in the lives of working-class people.[36] The ultimate silence for working-class women and men is that which derives from years of "hard labor and uncertainty," a "gradual silencing of dreams and the will to dream them."[37]

Addressing these silences from a feminist perspective, in "Beginning Where We Are: Feminist Methodology in Oral History," Kathryn Anderson and her colleagues note that when "women speak for themselves, they reveal hidden realities: new experiences and new perspectives emerge that challenge the 'truths' of official accounts and cast doubt upon established theories."[38] While interviewing a farm woman, Anderson asked about the respondent's hardships but then went awry by assuming that the woman's experiences could be generalized to those of other women in her community. "The two questions in succession have a double message: 'Tell me about your experience but don't tell me too much'"[39] The woman interviewed by Anderson failed to disclose personal information after that point. Her silence indicated that she would not generalize about others' experiences if the interviewer professed interest in her unique life history. The researchers in this study concluded that they must intrude less and offer fewer of their own preconceived interpretations that conformed to their theories. "We must learn to help women tell their own stories, and then learn to listen to those stories without being guided by models that restrict our ability to hear."[40]

In a similar fashion, Jill Taylor, Carol Gilligan, and Amy Sullivan in *Between Voice and Silence: Women, Girls, Race and Relationship*, report that differences in life experiences and backgrounds between the interviewer and respondents may silence some respondents because they do not believe that the interviewer can understand them free and clear of "controlling images or negative stereotypes."[41] They suggest that "who is listening may also influence what" respondents have to say.[42] Their findings may explain perceived differences between interviewers and respondents. "Adolescents may choose a form of political resistance—that is, choose not to speak about what they know and feel—to people they see as representing or aligned with unresponsive institutions and authorities, people who are for the most part from the dominant culture in the United States."[43] At times the disconnect is based on preconceived notions of difference and trust. "The degree of [a respondent's] protest that it is 'no problem' that her interviewer is [from another culture] may point to the fact that she chooses not to or feels it would not be safe or wise for her to say what she really thinks."[44]

A prudent silence was exercised by many of the women I interviewed and by those who chose not to be interviewed when I contacted them. Kim, now a union leader, did not relate any personal details about her life during her interview, choosing instead to talk about the strike, the company, and the union exclusively. While I may interpret her language and choice of words, I do not have an account of her childhood and her adult life. A self-described "need-to-know person," Kim likely had too few details about my project to feel comfortable talking about her life. Or she may not have seen the relevance of her life experiences to the study. Kim noted that her union experiences have given her much-needed knowledge to fight oppression, but she admitted that knowledge can be a burden as well. "A lot of issues, it gives you a headache, but I do the politics. Before I got in the union, I didn't pay attention to politics. But now I *know* what's happening in politics, what's happening around the world." Kim's omission may be her way of claiming knowledge for herself, given at her prerogative.

Ann Oakley, in "Interviewing Women: A Contradiction in Terms," examines the common practice of a masculine interview model that does not fit with feminist theory and may not work when interviewing women. Oakley states that the goal of interviewing is best achieved in a "non-hierarchical" dynamic in which the "interviewer is prepared to invest his or her own personal identity in the relationship."[45] The women she interviewed were eager to contribute to "'science' or for some book that many of the women interviewed would not read and none would profit from directly (though they hoped they would not lose too much)."[46] Oakley sought to reassure her respondents by engaging them in a "metaconversation" and by informing them that she "did not intend to exploit either them or the information they gave [her]."[47] Citing research in ethnography, Oakley points out that the opposition and barriers that some respondents may impose are the result of power relations. "Interviewees are people with considerable potential for sabotaging the attempt to research them."[48] Acknowledging that all research is political, Oakley insists that "personal involvement is more than dangerous bias—it is the condition under which people come to know each other and to admit others into their lives."[49]

Another reason that respondents may choose silence over giving voice to their lives and experiences is that they may feel that what they have to say may be too painful for the interviewer to hear. "If girls feel that 'no one ever listens,' perhaps it is because they are saying what no one wants to hear."[50]

> The girls in the study and the women in the retreats describe the enormous risks they feel in permitting themselves to be vulnerable—of being the subject of rumors and the gossip of their peers, of being rejected by colleagues or dismissed by authorities at work or school, of regenerating past hurts, of being overwhelmed by the needs of others, of feeling that they have betrayed members of their family or culture or class.[51]

In this research project, several women—Joan, Kim, and Millie—chose not to share many personal details about their lives. They may have had experiences that were too painful to discuss. In fact, Joan tearfully alluded to the pain she endured as a result of the strike. The self-protection and self-advocacy of these women highlight their power to resist institutional and individual encroachment and commodification. For others, the silences they claim may have a more powerful connotation. In her Nobel Prize acceptance speech, Toni Morrison invokes a silent wise woman to suggest the profundity of experience that silence reflects.

> And if the old and wise who have lived life and faced death cannot describe either, who can? But she does not; she keeps her secret; her good opinion of herself; her gnomic pronouncements; her art without commitment. She keeps her distance, enforces it and retreats into the

> singularity of isolation, in sophisticated, privileged space. Nothing, no
> word follows her declaration of transfer. That silence is deep, deeper
> than the meaning available in the words she has spoken.[52]

In this study, wise women claiming their status keep their own counsel,
choosing not to dilute their experiences with inadequate speech and reserv-
ing the power of their lives for themselves.

Silences also may derive from knowledge that is too painful to share.
In "The Drowned and the Saved," Susanna Egan compares the experiences
of Primo Levi and Paul Sternberg, both survivors of concentration camps,
noting that they recount different stories from the prisms of their memories, often painful to relate and to hear.

> Levi and many others have described the incredulity and distaste with
> which their stories were received. "I have often been reproached for
> remaining silent," says Levi's friend, Jean Samuel, "but the words
> wouldn't come. And who would have believed me?" The problems that
> Levi, Sternberg, and so many others recount with being heard, being
> tolerated, or being believed continue to reverberate into the twenty-first
> century and are far more complex than Holocaust denial. Most likely
> they do have to do with yet another aspect of human survival that
> comes at a cost; to extend our humanity, we must receive and attend to
> these things, but to live with ourselves on a daily basis, we need also to
> refuse the pain.[53]

Finally, Egan implies that silences are born of the necessity to survive; however, for the "survivor, the burden of knowledge is intolerable," especially
knowledge about oneself that is unacceptable or unlovable.[54] Therefore it
would be difficult, if not impossible, to share this burden with an interviewer who cannot begin to understand.

However, as Taylor and her colleagues suggest, "new pathways" of
learning about difference and bridging the gaps between people of various
cultures, classes, and generations will bring about new relationships and
new understanding.

> Exploring difference is about relationship. It is about bringing our-
> selves, again and again, to the edge of our not knowing, to the edge
> of our silences, to the edge of subjects that feel, and sometimes are,
> dangerous. Each time, we play out the drama of difference: when we
> reach that edge, when we come up to a moment of pain or confusion
> or impasse, what do we do? . . . To hold difference and sustain hope

requires us, moment by moment, to hold steady, to stay with ourselves and each other, to continue to learn how to speak in the presence of profound silences.[55]

This transcendence is possible. Ann Gill, in *Rhetoric and Human Understanding*, notes that people are powerless if they are compelled to be silent. She says, "We must learn to listen to all the voices, and individuals must find [authentic voices of their own]."[56] It has been my objective to listen to the authentic voices of the women in this project. With a number of the women who participated, I was able to bridge the gaps of age, race, culture, and class as the respondents gave voice to deeply personal, powerful experiences, sharing often tragic and painful events in their lives. Telling their stories, perhaps, will enable other women to find positive ways to resist oppression and patriarchy in interpersonal relationships and in their workplaces.

THE POWER OF HOPE AND RESISTANCE

Women who have been involved in labor disputes in North Carolina represent oppressed working-class women in the South. These women oppose injustice, sex discrimination, sexual harassment, and economic oppression in their families of origin, in their workplaces, in the corporate boardrooms, and in their unions. Their struggles continue as women in the state, around the country, and across the globe endeavor to combat oppression, social injustice, and poverty. Working-class women's narrative research should continue in order to share the message of resistance and hope to working women and men and to advance the cause of workplace democracy and union organizing.

Chapter Three
"Good as a Man": Identity [Re]formation in Male-Dominated Jobs

The social history of women working in traditional jobs for men encompasses the problems of sex-segregated jobs, pay inequity, sexual harassment, and gender discrimination. While most of the women in this study have worked in fields or jobs that traditionally have been considered to be the male domain, four of these respondents consider this to be the most significant aspect of their life narratives. These women's identities are constructed by their roles in male-dominated jobs, and this identification is the controlling idea of their narratives, forming the basis of their discourse community. They speak of the challenges and the triumphs that they have experienced in their working and personal lives. Historically, the impediments and the inequities that they face in the world of work have contributed to women's second-rate status and lack of economic and political power. For centuries, men in male-dominated fields have prevented women from access to these jobs and ultimately from realizing their power. As Hannah Arendt notes in *Crises of the Republic*, "power corresponds to the human ability . . . to act in concert. Power is never the property of an individual; it belongs to a group and remains in existence only so long as the group keeps together."[1] The respondents in this project report discrimination and degradation in their work in male-dominated fields. Despite these challenges, each woman's identity is situated within the context of her effectiveness and success in those roles that are conventionally assigned to men. I interviewed four women in the telecommunications and paper industries who strongly identify with their work in "men's jobs." Three of them were the first women to work in these positions, and they often faced harsh opposition, as did their sisters in the past.

The gender segregation of jobs in the United States explains to some extent the so-called wage gap wherein the earning capacity of women still lags behind that of men. In a 2003 article entitled, "Study Shows Gender

Wage Gap Has Widened," Marie Wilson noted, "Forty years after the Equal Pay Act of 1963, a new government report reveals we're moving backward on wage equality."[2] The wage gap is worse than it has been in recent decades, with women earning 44 percent less than men overall, with a difference of 21 percent when factors such as "childrearing and family responsibilities, as well as differences in women's education, occupations, and job tenure" are included.[3] Gender segregation is related to the wage gap. Nationally the number of women in non-traditional jobs continues to rise, but the rates are still very low. According to a report issued by the National Committee on Pay Equity, in 1992 women employed in the telecommunications industry were 8.2 percent of all "precision, production, craft, and repair workers" while women comprised 89 percent of telephone operators.[4] Ellen Bravo and Gloria Santa Anna note in "An Overview of Women and Work," that the discrimination that women have encountered at work has been ameliorated to a certain extent by laws enacted in the twentieth century; however, "women in this country still earn less than men for equivalent jobs."[5]

Women face other threats at work. "Many women today lose their jobs when they give birth. Sexual harassment remains a persistent problem [. . . and women] are woefully underrepresented in higher-paying positions."[6] While women comprise 46 percent of the labor force in the United States, 60 percent of women are primarily consigned to lower paying "service, sales, and clerical jobs."[7] According to a 2003 American Association of University Women report, *Women at Work*, "female workers remain segregated in what have been called 'pink-collar' fields [. . . with] nearly 30 percent of paid female workers in just 10 occupations. The majority of these are low-status service jobs such as receptionist, waitress, nursing aide, and cook."[8]

While pay inequities challenge women's success and independence, sexual harassment remains a persistent, degrading phenomenon in work environments. Julia Whealin, in "Sexual Harassment: An Overview of Its Impact for Women," reports that a 1981 survey of 24,000 government workers indicates that 42 percent of the women and 15 percent of the men surveyed "experienced sexual harassment."[9] Moreover, 52 percent of those who had experienced harassment had left their jobs or were fired as a result of the harassment. Whealin notes that women working in male-dominated and men working in female-dominated fields face the worst incidences of sexual harassment. "[W]orkers in settings composed predominately of the opposite sex tend to report higher rates of harassment than workers in occupations traditional for their sex."[10] According to Rosalyn Baxandall and Linda Gordon in their documentary history, *America's Working*

Women, the feminist movement is responsible for successfully putting sexual harassment on the agenda and for helping to criminalize this once-accepted behavior.[11] In the past women were forced to endure this practice. As one woman physician recalls from her medical school experience, it "was 'standard procedure' for professors to make 'male-female' jokes, usually genitally oriented, with the women bearing the brunt."[12] Women did not object because they wanted to succeed. "'What are you going to do, get up and walk out of class? You want to be a doctor? You want to be in a man's field? Then you swallow hard and pretend you don't hear.'"[13] The Equal Employment Opportunity Commission created new rules about sexual harassment in 1980, which were tested in the landmark 1986 Supreme Court case ruling that "sexual harassment did indeed violate civil rights."[14] Even though women are legally protected, they often fail to report sexual harassment because they fear that it will affect their jobs or prevent them from getting new positions if they pursue cases against supervisors and employers.

The pervasive problem of sexual harassment is not only degrading, it is also dangerous in certain fields. Baxandall and Gordon share the story of an anonymous female police officer whose story reveals demeaning and potentially deadly harassment.

> [A women's support group on the police force] got together to address the sexual harassment that was causing life-threatening situations on the street. For example, when you're calling in for help or you need backup and somebody cuts you off, or starts talking so you can't get through, or they don't show up when you call for help. Some of the men got tired of this too; they were getting cut off on the radio just because they were friends with or worked with one of the women. Until recently, harassment had been tolerated. But the chief took it seriously when we approached it as an officers' safety issue. Our point is that we should be able to do our jobs with mutual respect, and work in a safe environment where we can all get along.[15]

Another woman police officer told of a particularly degrading example of sexual harassment. "Louette Colombano was one of the first female police officers in her San Francisco district. While listening to the watch commander, she and the other officers stood at attention with their hands behind their backs. The officer behind her unzipped his fly and rubbed his penis against her hands."[16] When women enter a traditional field for men, the ensuing sexual harassment is just one way for men to assert their power—by demoralizing and undermining women in the workplace.

In the past women were subjected to an array of injustices, with sexual harassment being only one of them. In *Women Have Always Worked*, Alice Kessler-Harris notes that in sewing factories in the late 1800s, women often worked in unbearable sweatshop conditions.

> Women routinely worked ten hours a day, six days a week. Supervisors locked doors to prevent workers from going to the bathroom without permission. A variety of tricks cheated women of some of their meager wages. Employers turned back clocks to add extra minutes to the day or distributed tiny ticket stubs, easily lost, as tokens of work completed. Whispers of easy tasks in return for sexual favors filtered through the industry.[17]

The women's movement helped to bring these injustices to light and began steps to correct the problem, first by identifying the underlying causes. "Sexual harassment on the job . . . reflected the general perception of women as 'sex objects' who were not to be taken seriously in the world of ideas or work."[18]

"DOING A MAN'S JOB"

The historical challenges of women working in non-traditional jobs emerge in the narratives of the women in this research project. While the majority of the women in this study did work that is considered non-traditional for their gender, only a few of the respondents described their work as "doing a man's job." Of the four women in this study who construct their identities in part by their competition with men for higher-paying craft and technical positions, two work in the telecommunications industry, and two are former paper workers. All of the women have experienced discrimination in varying degrees, and all expressed the need to prove themselves to the men with whom they worked. In addition, the women spoke of the role their unions played in their successes and failures in the workplace; three of the four are very much pro-union but are inactive members of their locals. The fourth woman had a different experience when union members on at least two occasions harassed her and created additional stress; as a result, she is very much anti-union. Also, three of the four women had husbands who were supportive of their work, even taking on the more traditionally feminine roles of housework and child care to help their wives be more successful in their own work. Finally, these women spoke at length about their fathers' roles in their development as women who would be willing to take on non-traditional jobs in male-dominated fields. Like their sisters through the ages, North Carolina women doing the "work of men" are strong and capable, exuding confidence and pride in their work.

SALLY: FINDING HER STRENGTH THROUGH WORK

A thirty-six-year veteran in the telecommunications industry, Sally is an example of a worker who strongly identifies with her role as a woman in a "man's" job. She began her working life with the company as a junior college graduate seeking a summer job. She had planned to attend the university to complete her training as a prospective teacher; however, she found that she enjoyed her work as a telephone operator. "[My job] was as an operator, and it was working in the evenings. And they really needed somebody for that." Even though her decision to quit college to become a telephone operator angered her father, Sally reports that she wanted to continue working. "I *loved* that job. I *really* did" (her emphasis). Another important aspect of her work at that time was being able to work with people of another race. Since the local public schools and her junior college were segregated, Sally previously did not have the opportunity to associate with African Americans. She states, "[Working] was the first time I had ever been around black people. I had never gone to school with black people. And I'm only bringing this up because when I sat down at the cord board, the first person that I sat by was a really nice black girl." This point is relevant because the operators' long distance cords crossed each other, putting workers in close proximity with one another. On her first night of work as a greenhorn operator, Sally was learning, and she made mistakes. She spoke of one error that frightened her since it involved her new African American co-worker. "I pulled her cords down by accident, which is easy to do. And I was terrified because I really had never had any experience with black people. And I thought, 'Oh golly, she's gonna get really mad.' But she was so nice. Her name was Doris, and she really did help me a lot." From the beginning, Sally's positive experiences at work enabled her to find strength and autonomy.

The variety and novelty of her work were two additional reasons that Sally enjoyed her job as an operator. Soon after her employment began, she made the decision to forgo college and become a telecommunications worker permanently. She repeats, "I *loved* the job. It was great, and I worked evenings. But during that three months, there was a call for plant assigner." Sally was asked by her supervisor to apply for the position, but she declined. The woman completed an application for her, and Sally was offered the position. That reinforced her decision not to attend the university. "So she sent [the application] in. I got the job and went upstairs [to the new position] and made the decision not to go to [the university] because I loved it upstairs." Sally later remarked that the plant assigner position was the "highest-paying job that the prep people have." She says, "I was glad I made the move." Her decisions about working in the telecommunications field seem to be serendipitous even while her father was pressuring her to finish her education. "When I made the decision not to go, he was really mad about that." Since Sally's father was a demanding authoritarian, he was furious when he was defied. "He always expected me to do what he said, and it probably played a lot into why I decided to stay on there." At the age of twenty, Sally was experiencing her first rebellion against her father. Because she successfully defied her father, something she never expected to be able to do, Sally became confident, strong, and self-reliant. She notes, "I thought at the time that he's made all the decisions for me, it's time for me to do it. And I *can* do it. So throughout my career, I never felt like I couldn't do anything."

There Is Power in a Union

Later in her narrative Sally talks about another turning point in her career when her ignorance about the union was an impediment. As an assignment clerk in 1971, Sally had been employed with the company for two years when the union membership voted to strike. Since she had been from a non-union family with a father who was a manager at a local textile mill, Sally had no knowledge of the importance of union membership and solidarity with her fellow workers. Her lack of awareness became a painful and enduring lesson for the young woman. She recalls the experience:

> I still had not joined the union. But nobody really had ever asked me. When I went upstairs to the assignment clerk job, I was doing assignment work and there were two plant assigners. And they had a *lot* of [years of] service, and they were union members. But they never really approached me because I was young then, and you know, sort of like a kid. And I don't know why they didn't. Anyway, when the strike came about, I was working with one woman who was a union member and one who was not. The one who wasn't [a union member] told me, "Sally, you're not a union member, so you're not supposed to stay out or they can fire you because you're not a union member."

The woman went on to tell Sally to cross the picket line with her. Her co-worker said, "So you really should go across the line." Sally's lack of experience with the union and her failure to understand the significance of crossing the picket line were soon challenged by the events of the strike.

Sally recalls that at the time of the strike, "I didn't even know that you could sign up [with the union]." As if to apologize for her ignorance, she stated, "I know I sound awfully dumb, but I *was* young."

The scene of the picket line and the ensuing conflict are deeply ingrained in Sally's memory. She says, "We crossed the picket line and they were already out there. And that was the most traumatic thing I have ever gone through." Even though Sally has since endured the loss of her father and a beloved aunt, as well as conflicts with her older brother, crossing the picket line for four days in 1971 remains her most painful memory.

> The plant assigner I worked with was out there, and there was other people that I had worked with on the operator board and in engineering. I had worked with those people. And those people were out there too. And you know, they were hollering and things like that. When I went upstairs to work, I could look out the window and I could see them downstairs. They stayed out four days. And I will never forget it as long as I live. And that was a turning point for me. [When the strike ended], they came back [to work], and they were cold, which they should have been. And it took that experience for me to realize, you know, that they went out [on strike] for me too. And I signed my [union] card they day they came back.

Sally did not begrudge the striking workers their enmity toward her and the other employees who crossed the picket line. Rather, she felt that they were right and that she was wrong. "I could understand how they felt toward me. I've never got over it. I've never really got over that." Sally learned a harsh lesson that has had a lasting effect on her working life.

Solidarity on the Picket Line

In 1984 Sally was able to put her lesson into practice when the Communication Workers of America (CWA) again went on strike. The dispute was, as Sally recalls, "the best three weeks I ever had in my life." She was able to rectify her earlier wrong and to march on the picket line with her union sisters and brothers. "It was in August, and it was as hot as *could be*. My husband was working for the company then, and me and him had the best time in the whole world. We *really* did, that was the most fun we'd had [since] we didn't have any children then." While the other respondents of this study often recall the "good times" on the picket line, they remember the solidarity and camaraderie among the workers, but Sally expresses a deeper satisfaction with being a part of an event that would lead to improved working conditions for all workers. Since she felt that her ignorance during the 1971 strike was detrimental to her fellow workers when she "betrayed" them to cross the picket line, Sally could now show her support and kinship with the union and the common struggle. "I felt like a different person. I wouldn't have cared if we had stayed out [on strike] longer. And it didn't matter about the money because of that first time." In 1971 Sally had worked and had been paid, even, as she says, for "just four days" while her striking co-workers lost compensation for the same number of days. During her narrative, Sally returns again and again to her experience crossing the picket line:

> That was just such an eye-opener for me. And I'm so glad it happened because I feel like the union, especially where we work, has been so important. I make good money. I got good benefits, and I just really feel like there's people that went out on strike for me, and I got these benefits, and by not going out, I was saying, "Well, I'll let somebody else do my dirty work, but I'll reap from it."

Ultimately what Sally has reaped is a strong advocacy for the union. She now attends carefully to her co-workers and their union involvement, and she makes sure that she invites all new employees to join, explaining the benefits of union membership. In fact, when the company first employed her husband, Sally told him that he must join the union. She also told him about crossing the picket line. "I said under no circumstances would I encourage you to cross a picket line. I would tell [that to] anybody."

Sally's union participation and her solidarity with other CWA members extend in a different way to workers who are non-union and still benefit from the union. She says that every three years new contract negotiations with the company are fraught with controversy, and she closely observes her co-workers who are non-union. Sally's critical view of their "reaping the benefits" of the union while having "somebody else do their dirty work" reflects her early trauma.

> I'm always interested in who is not union members. And I wonder if they'll cross a picket line. And even *today*, if someone is not a union member, and they want to file a grievance, I don't feel good about that. I don't feel good toward them. I don't dislike them, and I don't mistreat them. Because I was treated cold, but yet nice, you know. And it took a long time for those feelings to get to where I didn't feel it. It was hard. At that age, I was in my twenties, and I think people maybe remember the ones that don't join the union. They just don't realize how emotional it is to cross the picket line.

Even though Sally acknowledges that unions have their negative aspects, she still remains a powerful and outspoken advocate, decades after her first experience with a strike.

However important the strikes and union involvement have been for Sally, much of her identity is derived from her work in a non-traditional field for women. Sally has worked in jobs that were considered to be the domain of men for more than half of her thirty-six-year tenure with the company. She credits the union with increasing the likelihood that these positions would be open to women. "If it hadn't been for the union, I don't think jobs would have been as available as they are for women." She goes on to report that her job is one that is difficult for women to attain. "I do hold a quote 'man's' job. In 1978 they set up negotiations to open up men's jobs to women *if* you could pass the tests." The tests for plant assigner and other traditional "men's jobs" were revamped and made more difficult; the previous test had been a simple, one-part assessment. Sally bid on a plant assigner position in 1984, fifteen years after she was first employed by the company. She had to complete a series of lengthy, increasingly difficult tests. "It was a six-hour test, and it was [in] four parts. It was really to weed out people. And I don't know if they timed it, but it was for women and minorities or what. You were put in a room with all these people to take it. If you failed the first part, they asked you to leave. You did not even get to go on. And after each part, people would get up and leave. Well, that's embarrassing."

Even though the tests were difficult, Sally passed all levels. She says that the personnel officer, a woman, was delighted that a woman finally passed the tests. "I made it. I made it all the way. After I went through all six parts, the lady from personnel, I never will forget it, she come out and hugged me, and she said, 'Thank God a woman passed it.' And she hugged me, and I will never forget that. I was the first woman to pass the stricter test." Eventually the position of plant assigner was phased out in the company, and Sally had to move twice to nearby towns to keep her position until she could bid on another male-dominated job, electronic technician (ET), a position she holds today. Sally had to retake the tests for this position, an achievement that was easy because of her previous working experience as a plant assigner. She notes that she was one of only a few women in the role of electronic technician. "When I come back to [town], I was the only woman ET in our district."

Moving into the male-dominated field of electronics technician led to Sally's conflicts with a male supervisor. Like her predecessors in the "man's domain," Sally soon learned that the discrimination and harassment that her sisters faced in earlier times remained in force. Her supervisor had years of working exclusively with men, and he obviously resented having to work with an electronics technician who was an intelligent, capable woman. Sally reports,

> I was the only woman ET, and he did not like women. He did not. He treated me really bad. And I thought that [the problem] was me at first, even though I've got a real good record, and I've got a real good memory also. And I could remember stuff really well so he'd only have to tell me [what to do] one time. And so I done really good work. But I thought his abuse was my fault. Then I found out that other women were complaining about him, clerical people and stuff like that. He dealt with, he treated women, really bad.

Initially Sally internalized the abuse of her supervisor as her problem, not his. She was accustomed to being treated fairly and having her work praised in all of her previous positions at the company. Her acceptance of this abuse may also be related to her demanding father and his impossibly high expectations. Sally states that her father "always expected a lot" from her. "My dad, for some reason, always got on me. He always expected me to make good, so I always made good grades because that's what he expected." Her father's domineering personality and behavior led Sally to question her competence as a child and later as an adult when she confronted a similar attitude in a supervisor.

Then Sally learned that this supervisor did not want women to have higher-paying jobs that "belonged to men." She said, "I found out that he had a thing [about] women. He didn't want women to be in higher jobs." She did not handle this pressure well at first. After she discovered that he was sexist, discriminating against her and other women employees, Sally decided to fight back. "At first I thought, 'Well, maybe I'm not doing right.' But then I started just sorta like talking back to him and standing up to him a little bit more. And then I seemed to get along better. So I think that if he could run over you, you were in trouble." When she decided to "stick to [her] ground," Sally learned that she could have both confidence in her work and deflect his abuse.

> I told myself that I know what I'm doing, which I felt like I did anyway. But I never said it to him. So I sort of got the feeling that maybe I just had to stand my ground and let him know, "Look, I'm a woman in this job, and I'm *doing* the job. And just because you are running the show doesn't mean that I have to put up with this." He made you feel like you were stupid, you know? Even though you knew you wasn't.

Sally eventually learned that ignoring him and standing up for herself were the most effective strategies for avoiding the abuse of her supervisor. Even today, Sally exhorts her female coworkers to fight the oppressive conditions of discrimination. "Let 'em know where you stand. They don't care. They think you're agreeing with everything if you don't say anything. They may think I'm a troublemaker, but so be it, you know?"

Sally admits that her courage to fight discrimination and oppression came late in her career. "I found my voice, but it's probably late. [The company] is certainly not like it used to be. Even though I found my voice, I don't think the union has the voice it once had. I think they're more in with the company now." She is still fighting for justice in a company that has, in her words, "deteriorated" and "gone backwards." She also thinks that workers are not as dedicated as they once were. She acknowledges that grievances take longer to settle, and the union is conceding more and more in conflicts with the company. In addition, the company is not like "family" as it once was. Sally states that she once believed that she had the "best job in the world," but that today she would not make that claim. One reason for her disillusionment came five years ago when her son-in-law applied for a position in the company during a hiring campaign. He passed all the tests and quit his other job in anticipation of being hired. Meanwhile a hiring freeze went into effect, and he was told that he would not get a job with the telecommunications company. Sally became very angry because he was without employment, and she had encouraged him to apply at the phone company. She attempted to rectify the situation herself.

> I got on the phone and called my second level [supervisor]. I actually cried and everything, I was so upset. And I said, "You know, look, I recommended this company to him. And you see what they done." Well, a week went by, and I didn't get any satisfaction from them. So I got on the phone and I called the vice-president of the company myself. And do you know, he answered the phone? I was so shocked, I was speechless. And I finally said, "Mr. [___], I want to tell you about this guy that I recommended to come to work here because I thought it was the greatest company in the world. Do you know how I feel being an employee with 31 years? I feel like dirt. He has no job! I don't think [this company] should have done that to him, and I want you to do something about it if you can."

Sally later learned that the vice-president called the personnel office in Atlanta and had the job reinstated. Sally was relieved that her tactic worked. She said, "So you *can* go up through the ranks and you *can* get satisfaction.

The union did not get his job. I didn't even go to the union. I felt this was a company matter."

Even though she chose not to involve the union in her son-in-law's case, Sally remains an enthusiastic supporter of the CWA, crediting the union with opening jobs for women that previously were held only by men. In addition, she states that the union is also responsible for the excellent benefits that she enjoys, including an impending retirement with benefits that will take care of her in later life. To highlight the union's effectiveness, Sally cites an example of her husband's successful grievance after losing his position during a lay-off. When the year-long furlough ended, he did not regain his previous job even though he was clearly entitled to it. He asked the union to represent his case, and eventually he was restored to his former job. Since Sally is cynical about the company's motives with respect to workers, pay, and benefits, she hopes that the unions can continue to fight effectively for workers' rights. "My work experience as a woman with a union company has been great. I do hope unions stay strong because workers need somebody to stand up for them. You need a place to go and grieve things that you see are wrong. And you need support." Finally, she returns to her early experience during the strike of 1971. "When we had the strike, and I crossed the picket line, I learned that everybody needs to stand together to make things better for all." For Sally, unions are essential to a democratic work environment.

In addition to the support that she felt from the union, Sally also ben-efited from having a husband who was completely supportive of her work-ing life. During his year-long layoff, Sally's husband cared for their infant daughter exclusively and did all the housework while Sally worked. "He kept [our daughter] a whole year." While she worked, her husband took care of the household. "He done everything. He babysat; he changed every diaper. I never changed a diaper. I never cooked a meal, and I never cleaned house for a solid year. My daughter didn't have anything to do with me." While her overbearing father and her demanding, sexist supervisor may have attempted to oppress Sally with their limiting behaviors, she enjoys an egalitarian mar-riage with a man who is both capable in the traditional feminine roles of housekeeping and childcare and also supports his wife's career. This element in Sally's success is reflected in the lives of other women in this study. Sally continues to be a dedicated unionist and capable worker whose lengthy career is a testament to her fortitude and persistence.

SUZANNE: MANY "FIRSTS" FOR A WOMAN

Suzanne, a Paper, Allied Chemical, and Electrical (PACE) union member from a mountain county, is another working woman who defines herself as a pioneering woman in roles traditionally open only to men. In 1963, when she completed high school, Suzanne's first job in the paper mill was in the finishing department where previously only men were hired for the heavy work. However, the company recently had added new features to equalize the labor, and Suzanne was the first woman to operate the "slitter" machines that cut the paper. She says, "It was hard work, but I still was able to do it." Throughout her career with the company, Suzanne was the first woman employed in what were previously male-only positions on four separate occasions. Indeed, while she faced discrimination and personal difficulties, Suzanne eventually managed to be promoted to increasingly higher-paying and intellectually challenging jobs that previously were available only to men. She even battled breast cancer and returned to a physically demanding job during her recovery. Following the closing of the paper mill in 2001, Suzanne has devoted herself to serving young people through a local service organization, another male domain. Suzanne was the first woman to join the club, and she hopes to bring more women into the group. She is the state chairperson of an international exchange group within the organization, another example of her quest for challenge and service. She told me that she decided to "go ahead and do it [join the club], and then the other girls would come in." Suzanne's greatest strengths are her determination to integrate the once-barred worlds of men and her commitment to her family, her work, and her community.

Though she began work at the paper mill in a "man's job," Suzanne left the company to find day-shift work at another plant when her children were small. When she returned to the paper mill several years later, Suzanne worked in the winding department. She notes, "I did a man's job. I mean, it was heavy lifting and all." Suzanne did this work until 1994 when she was diagnosed with breast cancer. She went back to work as soon as possible, but her job in the winding department was too demanding for a woman whose breast and underarm lymph nodes had been removed. "It was *very* hard to go back and lift all that stuff and everything, so I got out of winding and went back to finishing." After a few months, Suzanne learned about an opening at the boiler house. "And no woman had ever worked over there, now. And I said, 'I can't do that.' And then I said, 'But what have I got to lose?' So I thought, I'm gonna try it. So I did, and some of the men resented it." The men's opposition forced Suzanne to prove herself once she got into the boiler house position. After they saw that she could indeed handle the heavy labor involved in the job, Suzanne says that their attitude changed. "I mean they respected me because I would not have done it if I could not do the job. I saw that I could do it even though I had had breast cancer, and I still had a weak arm. I could still do it." Her strength is even

more admirable considering that her transition to the boiler house occurred
during a series of personal crises.

Surviving Hardships

Suzanne's mastectomy occurred in March 1994, and three family members
died within a year of her health crisis. As if that were not enough to endure,
Suzanne's daughter left for college during the fall of that year, and Suzanne
was without her daughter's emotional support. She tells of the year's rav-
ages that left her physically and emotionally scarred.

> My aunt died from [cancer]. My first cousin died from it. And this is all
> breast cancer. But my dad died of lung cancer. My husband's dad died
> of lung cancer, too. So they both died in the year of 1994. I had breast
> cancer in March. My mother-in-law died in July, and my sister died in
> October. And I had to change jobs that year. My mother had a stroke
> in December, and she give up. We seen her give up because of my sis-
> ter. We know it's because of my sister. And she died in February 1995.
> All that just in [such a short time] and my daughter had went away to
> school too. It was a really hard, hard year.

Suzanne's work challenges were made even more difficult to bear by the
trauma she experienced in the many losses during one terrible year; however, she is not merely a survivor, she is a triumphant and contented person
who has overcome many difficulties.

The endurance that Suzanne demonstrated during her personal trials served her again when she accepted another position in the province
of men. When a position in the filtration department became available,
Suzanne applied for and got the job. As she reports, this work was not only
physically challenging, it was also mentally demanding. She was required to
attend classes and become licensed in water treatment and wastewater control. "And that was one of the best jobs in the company, and another thing,
there's never no woman ever worked up there, you know." She is proud of
her series of ground-breaking promotions as a woman in non-traditional
roles for women. However, Suzanne emphasizes that she did not pursue
these jobs because of that fact alone. "I didn't go because I'm a woman. I
went because it's a job, and if you took the job, you got the pay." Again,
she informed me that she would not have taken the job if she could not
have done the work. "I would *not* have done that if I could not carry my
load."

When I asked her about pay equity between men and women in the
same job, Suzanne was quick to reply that "there was no difference in your

pay." She went on to say, "If there's a man working beside of you, he gets the same pay you get. [Men] never got more money than we did if we were doing the same job." The wastewater treatment job was the best position that Suzanne ever held, and she took pride in doing good work. An added bonus was that the pay was excellent. "That was the best-paying job I've ever had. And it was all men up there, but they treated me with respect." The men begrudgingly accepted Suzanne, and while they may have respected her, they also delighted in frightening her. "I went down to the pump house, and the guy that took me down there was the operator then. Later he would be my supervisor. He come out with [a snake] wrapped around his waist. And if I could've got the car, I would have left him down there." The men may have been trying to intimidate her or to make her reconsider working in the filtration department. No matter the intent, the outcome was that Suzanne worked in that department until her forced early retirement when the paper mill closed in 2001.

As in Sally's case, Suzanne's father had an important role in shaping her work experiences; however, unlike Sally, Suzanne's father was a positive model for hard work and competence. He also worked at the paper mill and helped Suzanne get her first job there. Moreover, he provided Suzanne with experiences that helped her to develop confidence and believe in her strength and capabilities. She contrasts his influence with that of her mother; though she says little about her, Suzanne's comments are veiled criticisms. "My mother never did work. I say 'never did work.' She was a stay-at-home mom." Changing her voice to a hearty, enthusiastic tone, Suzanne's next commented, "My dad was a *very* hard worker. And he worked at the plant." She goes on to tell about his work ethic. "And he was one that didn't miss work. You don't stay out to go somewhere and call in sick." Suzanne continues to tell his story, emphasizing painful details.

> My dad didn't miss very many days until he got cancer. In fact, he'd never been in the hospital or anything until he got cancer. And he had lung cancer. I would say he was seventy-six years old the first time he went to the hospital. And it was because he had lung cancer. He was a hard worker and everything. And see, back then, my whole family worked at the plant at one time except my mother. Everybody else has been [at the mill] at some time.

Suzanne's narrative has minimal commentary about her mother, and this raises questions about her opinions. Perhaps her lack of respect for her mother's work is as responsible for Suzanne's working life as is her admiration of her father's devotion to his work. Since she disparages her mother's role as a homemaker, it is reasonable to expect that Suzanne likely would find great satisfaction in her own successes in the "man's world" of work.

Suzanne also speaks of her husband's support and encouragement in all of her endeavors, another parallel to Sally's story. During the strikes of 1974 and 2001, Suzanne's husband was a member of management at the paper mill where she also worked. He crossed the picket line while Suzanne marched in solidarity with her union sisters and brothers. She says, "He had to go in because he was a supervisor, and I was union. And I walked the picket lines, and it wasn't nothing against him." He was as understanding of her union responsibilities as well, being supportive of her actions. "Because he knew I had a job to do, and he had a job to do." Their differences during the strike were not an obstacle for the couple. Indeed, they have a strong relationship and support one another in any endeavor or difficulty. She praised her husband's encouraging nature.

> Never has he ever told me anything about where I work or anything. He supported me. He never would say, "Don't go. Don't do that." He always supported me in all my decisions wherever I worked. Even after he left the paper mill, and I was still there, and if I wanted to work overtime, which I worked a *lot* of overtime there, you know. If I called and said, "I'm gonna work over tonight," he always supported me in my work.

Throughout their married life, this couple has endured work challenges and personal difficulties, but their bond is as strong as their wills to survive. Today, they both are active in a local service organization, with Suzanne having joined her husband's all-male club with his encouragement and support.

After Loss, a Miracle

Through all of this family's losses, they also experienced what she calls a miracle, an event that sustains Suzanne in her daily life. Though relatively silent about her childhood and the strikes, she was eager to get past what she perceived was the "real" interview about her working life and the strikes at the paper mill. When she had concluded her narrative about work, Suzanne proceeded to tell me about her son who survived an automobile accident when logically he should not have. Late in 2001, he was driving to Charleston to visit his girlfriend and her parents when the accident occurred.

> This is Labor Day weekend, and you know traffic is bumper to bumper, and he had a wreck. He started to go around this car, and when he did,

there was a car in his blind spot. So I mean, he's going seventy miles an hour. He flips back and loses control. He's on the side of the road. He gets off the road and knows he can't get back on because he's gonna involve a lot more traffic. And he don't have his seatbelt on. . . . He starts flipping. He has the window down. . . . So he comes out of the truck, and the truck [flips over him] and lands at his feet.

Suzanne's son had five broken ribs and a punctured lung. His dog was thrown from the vehicle. Though unhurt, the animal ran away from the scene. Two miles from the accident, another driver caught the dog. The woman who rescued the dog had a child who is usually afraid of dogs, but not this time. "And this girl calls the dog and he comes over to her car. She's got a little four-year-old boy who's *horrified* of dogs. And this is a boxer, you know."

Suzanne makes much of the coincidences and the fortuitous outcome of the accident: the woman who finds the dog lives only thirty minutes away from her son's home and though usually frightened, her son played with the dog. In addition, the first car to get to the accident scene contained emergency medical technicians who took care of her son while they waited for the ambulance. She repeats that her son's escape from certain death is nothing short of a miracle. "For him to come out of that with the truck going over the top of him and landing at his feet. My knees get weak every time I think about it." After enduring years of hard work, illness, loss, and grief, Suzanne chooses to focus on what she calls a "good thing," the fact that her son is living and working. She chooses to focus on the good life that remains. Suzanne is a happy, active person who survives after the closure of the paper mill, the loss of so many loved ones, and the near misses that make her grateful.

NAOMI: "BETTER THAN THE BOYS"

Naomi is another PACE union member, a determined woman whose working life has included a number of jobs that previously were reserved for men. At age eighteen, just after she married her childhood sweetheart, she began working at a local thread factory in a typical job for a woman. However, she considers her first "real job" to be when she began to work in the paper mill alongside her husband in jobs that were typical for men. During her tenure at the plant, which spanned from 1967 to 2001, Naomi worked in the finishing department, then moved into maintenance, and finally earned her electrician's license. Throughout her working life, she has exhibited the confidence, intelligence, and determination to gain jobs that once were designed for men. During the interview, Naomi showed me her licenses and training certifications, all of which attest to her diverse skills and abilities. As with Suzanne, Naomi has endured physical challenges that currently limit her employment opportunities after the loss of her job when the plant closed in 2001. And as with her PACE sister, Naomi has benefited in both her personal and working lives from having a supportive, involved husband and a strong, capable father who fostered independence and confidence in his daughter, helping her to know that she could do anything that she attempted.

Discrimination and Layoffs

In relating her work narrative, Naomi laughingly recalled that she intended to work only until she and her husband "got on their feet" financially, but that they always needed additional income for their family. As she says, "the more you have, the more you want." In other words, both she and her husband expected that their family would reflect the traditional model of a working husband and a stay-at-home mother. However, Naomi worked continuously except for a brief period several months before and for several weeks after her son was born. When she went to work at the paper mill, Naomi immediately encountered the sex segregation that exists in many industries. "When I went to work, and this is odd; people find this hard to believe. They had two seniority lists in each department, a women's and a men's. They had what they considered men's jobs and they had what they considered women's jobs." Later on, management began to correct this discriminatory practice. "I guess you'd call it affirmative action to correct mistakes that had been made over there. They combined the two seniority lists, and they tried to slot you in when you came back to work. It really didn't work out. One of my friends that worked there wound up having seniority over a *man* that was working there the day she was *born*. Eventually it did all work as people retired." Naomi worked at the paper mill for two years before she became pregnant with her son and was forced out on maternity leave.

> At that time when you were pregnant, you *had to quit* at six months. There was a *law* that said in the industry that women could not work beyond six months. In the earlier days a lot of the women who went out on maternity leave, they hired them back. But you had a certain length of time that you held your recall rights [which] held your seniority. It didn't happen to me, but a lot of the women swore to the fact that two days after their time ran out, they'd call and say, "We're ready for you to come back; we've got an opening if you wanna come back."

> Of course they had to start out brand new, seniority all over. Over the
> years [the government] made them change that.

The unfair practice of penalizing pregnant women and mothers was just
one injustice that led the workers to campaign for a union. The first vote
was in 1969 when Naomi was pregnant. "The first one I remember voting
in was in July of 1969. I waddled in pregnant as can be. I was out, [but]
they had to let me vote because I still had not lost my seniority rights at that
time." The eventual success of the organizing campaign led to improved
conditions for the women workers.

Equity in "Men's" Jobs

At about the same time as the union election, the paper industry was experiencing a downturn. Several departments closed entirely, and others lost
positions. When they brought Naomi and other workers into the finishing
department, they combined the seniority lists, and "those jobs that used to
be typical *men's* jobs, some women had to take them." This was a boon
for Naomi who does not avoid hard work. She stated, "I could do as good
as men." This job worked well for Naomi until her son was born. At that
time she experienced difficulty with childcare because of the twelve-hour
"swing" shifts. "It's hard to keep babysitters when you work shifts." Therefore Naomi decided that she should seek an office job on the first shift since
the company had a policy of hiring from within the plant before seeking
applicants from outside. "I went to school for everything you can think
of for women, back in those days. I caught up on my shorthand. Typing.
Little bit of accounting skills. That's basically all women did in those days
in an office." Naomi applied for several office jobs within the company, but
when she learned about the dress code, she changed her mind. "In the '70s
and '80s, when you went to work in an office, you *dressed*. People had to
spend more than they made [on clothes for work.] So I turned them down.
Because if you are spending more than you make at that job, you need to
find another job." However, this did not solve Naomi's childcare dilemma
and the shift work requirements of her job.

> I decided right after that that we had some men that came in and
> worked on machines and some of 'em, I mean, a moron could of done
> what they was doing. So I decided I'd get me one of those maintenance
> jobs. I kept puttin' in for 'em 'cause they posted those also. And every,
> *every time*, without fail, I'd get a little letter, a form letter, back. It
> always started out, "Thank you for your interest, *but* so-and-so got the
> job." I called them "Thank you, but" letters. I mean it was actually a

joke in the department. One day, I decided, the laws are changing, and they're gonna have to take some women. Well, I decided that I was gonna go get training and be ready when that day come along.

With this realization, Naomi began to acquire the training that would eventually lead to nearly a dozen certifications and diplomas as an industrial electrician.

Training for the "men's jobs" was conducted jointly by the plant and the union, but Naomi credits the union for insisting that women be included in the classes. Naomi enrolled in classes to gain various skills, but as she says, "I'm gonna get me a day job. And if some of these men can do these things, I can." She got another job doing mechanical work. Initially this was a challenge to her husband's work and status. "My husband was a millwright. Mechanical work was much harder, heavier work. Heavier duty work than he was doing." After her first class with the union, her husband said, "'No, no, that's what *I* do.'" He said, "'You can't stand up to that physical labor.'" However, her husband's protests did not deter her. Naomi notes that two women took the training. She coyly says that "one woman made it; the other one didn't," implying that *she* was the successful woman in that first training. Later she attended a second class, Electrical Instrumentation and Heating, Ventilation, and Air Conditioning (HVAC.) "They chose ten of us. We went in; we had no earthly idea at the end of the year what we would even be doing, but it would be one of those jobs. You got your *pick* of the jobs." Nevertheless the competition for the jobs was fierce. "You had tests twice each week; you had the job test every month. They scored those. By the end of the year, whoever had the highest average got the first choice of whatever [job] was there. I wasn't number one; I was number three out of ten." Naomi's third place standing is misleading since her average was as she still recalls, "98.13." She says that "no one had a [score of] ninety-nine. We were all within hundredths of each other." Though he was initially against the idea of Naomi working in maintenance, her husband eventually understood that his family's progress and happiness depended on Naomi's freedom to do any work she chose. In addition to his work at the paper mill, her husband is a volunteer fire-fighter, an important role in his life. As Naomi stated, "He actually took that first year off from fire training so he could help baby-sit so I could score high [on the tests]."

After her training and testing, Naomi earned a position as the first woman electrician at the company, working the day shift as she had desired. This highly skilled technical job in a traditional male field led her to discover her analytical capabilities. The job also entailed preventive maintenance of the motors and electrical systems of the plant, which at that time employed nearly 3000 people. "At first, one person did not go everywhere. They divided it into areas [of responsibility.] Then they made us take a turn through *all* the mill, make sure you at least got around once. And I did motors. I handled all the motors for the whole union."

Naomi enjoyed the work that challenged her mentally and physically. She did troubleshooting on broken motors to determine the problems and then wrote orders for repairs, which were done by an outside vendor. When the motors had been repaired, Naomi checked them in and approved them for use. "I had to check [the motors], run them to make sure that they were working." Her analytical skills were honed during the process.

> Why does that same motor, it might be used in ten different applications, why would it not run over there for so long? And maybe it'd run over here forever. Three or four times longer. What's wrong with that application? Does it need a bigger motor? Does it need a smaller motor? Is it hooked up to the wrong pulley? Is it lined up? You're trying to figure out what's causing failure because you don't want to be standing there longer than you have to.

Naomi understood the significance of her work and took great pride in her abilities. As she says, "This was just an *important* job because if the motors don't run, that place don't run."

A staunch union member, Naomi also credits the union with affording her the opportunity to do a "man's" job. The union set up the schools and training courses for the various skilled jobs and invited women to apply in order to gain access to the jobs traditionally reserved for men. Naomi states that the union "actually encouraged women to join maintenance." However, the stigma attached to being the first woman in a higher-paying, male-dominated field was often difficult for Naomi. She reports that the discrimination and sexism were apparent early in her career as an electrician. "It's odd being the only woman in a big bucket. Most of the men can only see us as women. And at first some of their wives didn't want their husbands working with a woman." Naomi knew that she would have to make subtle inroads into their domain. "I tried when I sit down at break time or lunch time, whatever, I tried not to make them feel uncomfortable. I mean they worked there, too." On the other hand, she would not allow them to make disparaging or sexist remarks in her presence. "I didn't take nothing off of none of them. I mean I can put you in your place without opening my mouth. I have what my husband calls the 'evil eye.' I mean I can give as good as I get. I prefer not to, but I *can*. Like I said, when I came along, it turned out no longer to be a good old boys' club." While she was asserting her right to work in the "good old boys' club," Naomi was also negotiating how to manage the heavy lifting in her job, among other difficulties. She was adamant that if a woman accepts a job, she should be capable of doing it. "If you ask us to do what's traditionally called a man's job, you oughta be prepared to do what you have to do to earn the same money." At first she was unable to seek assistance from her co-workers because of this deeply-rooted notion of independence. However, she later changed her mind. "I then never felt bad about asking for help. The men ask for help. It probably took me longer to ask for help than it would a man. I didn't want to ask for help if I could [avoid] it."

Naomi's independent streak, together with her confidence and strength, are the result of early childhood lessons when she was trained to be a hard-working, persistent individual. The oldest of eight children, Naomi grew up in a small mountain town in a family that scrabbled for existence in the unpredictable farming and logging trades. Naomi's father encouraged his children to be confident, capable, determined, and ethical—as he was—even in the face of bitter business disappointments.

> My daddy was in World War II and the Korean War. When he came out, first he logged and pulped wood. He did really good up until the year we had so many snows. It snowed every Thursday in '59 or '60. My daddy had eight men that worked for him. And he owned a majority of this road. And they all worked at the [logging] camp. They all hauled logs to the camp. A lot of the days you could go to the woods and cut it, get it on the ground ready to load, but you couldn't get the trucks in to load and haul it out. My daddy paid those men *every week*. They worked when they could work. My daddy paid them faithfully, " 'cause they got little young 'uns," I can still hear him saying. My daddy was good to everybody, and it wound up that he lost basically everything he had.

After his logging business failed, Naomi reports that her father had to "go get an actual job, do public work." He became a prison guard until the state closed the local prison. The family could have moved to Raleigh so that her father could work in the prison there, but he chose to stay in their home community. "It's different when you've got eight kids and a wife trying to make it on what a prison guard makes. And you've got to rent a house [in Raleigh]." Finally, her father found work at the local textile mill where Naomi herself would later work at her first job. His position there was as an electrician. Her father's lessons of hard work and persistence in the face of defeats as well as his work as an electrician likely motivated Naomi to take on a nontraditional job years later.

Her childhood experiences deeply influenced the worker and the woman that Naomi would become. As she notes, her father relied on her as the oldest child to set the example and to work harder than the rest of the children. Her work in the fields helped support the family's "sideline" business of "truck farming," where, from the back of a truck, the family sold vegetables that they had grown. Naomi was also expected to chop and carry wood for heating and cooking. Her father's expectations were always high, and he enforced them with praise. "My daddy told me many times that I was the best field hand he had. He wasn't putting down my brothers, but like I say, I could do it." She acknowledges her strength while also noting the sex segregation and inequality within a household that included five brothers and two sisters.

> I mean, I can set out cabbage; I can hoe corn. I can do it as good as any of the boys. We had a wood stove, that was our kitchen stove. I could split wood and carry it in. But when we got home, daddy and the boys sat down and rested. And you know what the girls had to do. They had to help Mama get the meal on the table, clean up the kitchen. My mama had eight kids, so there was always somebody needing something. We had to do all that.

Naomi's work ethic, endurance, and capabilities were not the only lessons learned from her father. He encouraged her to try her best and to succeed in all endeavors. As she says, "My daddy never told me I couldn't do [something]." Later on, she admits that if she ever expressed doubt in her abilities or said, "I can't," he would reply: "'Can't never could and never will.'" This early lesson figures directly into her decision to join the maintenance team. "Nobody told me I couldn't. I'll be honest; when I went into maintenance, and I went to work down there, *I got to work*. I don't mind working. I might as well make all I can while I'm there." Indeed, this decision is both personal and economic, as Naomi points out, "Why work for six dollars an hour when you can get ten dollars?" She is as pragmatic as she is proud of her accomplishments.

The loss of Naomi's job was a major turning point for a woman who enjoys work and achievements. Naomi worked diligently for the union during the strikes and endeavored to improve the conditions of their labor for her fellow workers. In 1971, during the first strike, she walked the picket line for herself and her husband for six weeks since he had a part-time job that they needed to support their young family during the strike. However,

Naomi and her husband both were supportive of the union and the strike, so they thought it was important that at least one of them would take both turns on the picket line. They both believed in the power of the union. For example, Naomi praises the safety advances that unionization brought to the company. Because of the PACE guidelines, workers were required to wear safety glasses, ear plugs, and appropriate safety shoes and clothing. Prior to that, Naomi says, she often went to work in shorts and sandals. In addition to safety, the union brought real bargaining power to the workers. In 2001, while the union fought the drastic pay and benefits cuts proposed by the new company owner, Naomi and her co-workers learned that their strike was a failure. Refusing to bargain in good faith, the owner closed the company, as he had threatened early in the negotiations. Naomi said the cuts that he proposed were criminal. Instead of the promised 10 percent pay cut, the company would take up to 60 percent of workers' pay. "I set down and figured mine up, and I was gonna lose 49.5 percent." As Naomi states, "There was *no* give and take. So it sorta ended up a stalemate."

Overall Naomi will also lose 60 percent of her retirement funds, a loss that occurred because she had only six additional months of work until she would be fifty-five years old. At that age, she would have lost only 10 percent of her retirement benefits. In addition to the tragic loss of jobs for the community, many older workers like Naomi face drastic losses in their pensions. Moreover, Naomi was unwilling to retire for another reason.

> I mean, I worked long and hard. The biggest problem is that I won't be able to find another job. I've had two [ruptured] brain aneurisms, August 5, 1998 and August 13, 1998. But the Lord's been good to me. I had surgery twice. There's about six weeks after the second surgery that I do not remember. They say up until the second surgery that I knew everything. I was still in the hospital when the second one happened. And I had to go to rehab.

The difficulties she faced in rehabilitation could not prepare her for what the company would do when she returned. Because someone died in the plant during her hospital stay, the company was leery of allowing someone with aneurisms to return to a dangerous job. Naomi wanted to work. "I fought to go back to work, 'cause I could have went out on disability. I don't want to be disabled. I want to work." The state sent someone to evaluate Naomi's fitness for the job, and they declared that she was capable of working. Naomi showed me the report and joked, "I have papers that show I've got good sense."

However, now that the mill is closed, Naomi will not be able to find another job because of her medical history. As she says, "I'm gonna have trouble finding another job in my field as an electrician." She went on to say that even she would not hire someone with a history of aneurisms because it is "very, very dangerous" work. She has considered residential electrical work instead of industrial, but noted that "this county's overrun with them," and she would also have to get different licenses and attend school every year. Naomi's story of loss is linked with that of her mountain community since the paper mill was the primary employer in the county. More than 1000 people were working at the mill at the time of its closing, and many other businesses depended on the incomes of the now-unemployed workers. She says of her company that it "was a good place to work. I worked at the same place for thirty-five years." Naomi and her co-workers, two years into their unemployment, face the challenges of crafting new lives for themselves after the paper mill closed.

LYNDA: INTEGRATING THE TELECOMMUNICATIONS WORKFORCE

One of the women in my study, Lynda, a veteran in the male-dominated telecommunications industry, faced a multitude of difficulties when she first took a repair technician position in a local company. Hired in 1978, in an action forced by the Federal Communications Commission, Lynda was one of two women hired along with two African American men to integrate the utilities workforce. During the past twenty-five years, Lynda's work has been fraught with discrimination, sexual harassment, hostilities, and dangerous working conditions, as well as overbearing, sexist, and cruel supervisors. For the first fifteen years of her work, Lynda suffered from being an outsider who was openly disliked and whom the men would try to force out of the company through systematic, persistent harassment.

Lynda describes the hostile work environment she encountered. "Number one, the men didn't want us. At all. We weren't talked to, except down to." She recounts her first job training experiences with a sexist male instructor.

> He was your typical old man, never had women out there; women were meant to be barefoot and pregnant, nothing else, but by God, they had nice butts! You know? And if he could cop a feel of a nice butt, then so be it. You would be coming down off a pole and by the time you get seven feet off the ground, he'd grab you by the cheeks, and he'd say, "You've got to swing, baby! You've got to swing!" and he'd be swinging your rear end left and right, and you're trying desperately to keep your feet on that little pole.

Her later experiences with male supervisors and co-workers detail even more blatant sexual harassment and dangerous working conditions. When she was assigned to a dangerous neighborhood, working alone where no man was expected to work solo, Lynda was attacked by a mob of young men. "I'm shaking. I'm screaming like hysterical screams. I'm getting beat in the head and the back and everywhere. He has a knife." She later told her supervisor, "You keep me over there working by myself, I'm going to get killed."

While her supervisors and co-workers harassed and demeaned her, the union offered no solace; instead it added to her work woes. When she began working with her union local as a volunteer, Lynda was demoralized by the local president's suggestion that she "entertain" a visiting national vice-president and be paid for sexual favors with union money. She refused, resigning her union membership though she was later ostracized for doing so. Lynda told a co-worker who questioned her decision, "I'm not going to prostitute myself and be paid out of my union dues!" She relates the story of her co-workers' hostility after she quit the union. "It was like somebody shut a door. I went to work, and it was like the wall. They didn't speak. They didn't acknowledge that I was there. If they bumped into me, it wasn't 'Excuse me.' It wasn't *anything*. Therefore, the union, also dominated by men, effectively silenced this woman worker, enforcing gender inequality through sexism, sexual harassment, and discrimination.

Unlike Suzanne's and Naomi's experiences with supportive fathers, Lynda's life in her family of origin was less than ideal. For her, home was not a haven. She lived with a demanding, controlling, and cruel father, and she fought back only when she could do so with hope of success. Lynda's narrative begins at age eleven when she tells the story of running away from home after hearing her parents argue as they often did. When she heard her father say, "If it wasn't for the kids, I would be out of here," Lynda's response to that was:

> Well, I knew my mother—my mother was with me and my brother, he's two years older than me—I knew he was her favorite, and I thought, well, I'll get out of here. They'll split up, they'll be happy. I was eleven years old; that was my logic. I packed my little bags, you know. I walked eleven miles. I walked across the Yadkin River—there was a place with cracks in the bridge, you could hear the water sliding around.

When she woke up after spending the night outdoors, she smelled breakfast cooking in a nearby house, so she knocked on the door. She would not tell the man who she was, but when asked about her Bible, she told him: "I got like nine years perfect attendance at church, I can't miss church now. I ain't gonna be at home, but I can't miss church. So he asked me who my preacher was, and I told him."

The man's trick gave him enough information to find Lynda's father. As she tells of his arrival, her story turns even darker, revealing one origin of two persistent elements in her narrative: independence and self-determination. When her father arrived, he was not glad to see her. Instead, he focused on browbeating Lynda into submission.

> And instead of the loving huggy type—my dad wasn't—when he was angry, you could forget that, okay? He took each article out of my suit-case, outside, made me stand outside in the snow and ice, and he said, "I bought this, I paid for this, so I'm throwing it away. Let me tell you something. When you leave this house, you will take with you only what you own and nothing else. And you will work for what you get." Boy, that made an impression on me like nothing you couldn't believe. I was terrified. And I never forgot that.

This fear coexisted with the empathy Lynda has for animals since her father would never nurse a sick pet or take it to a veterinarian. Lynda could not get love from her mother and father, so she got it from her pets. However, her father was as cruel to animals as he was to his children. Lynda says, "So I had my animals—it was all I had to play with. When one was sick, he wouldn't take it to the vet. I would have to lay and watch it suffer and die, okay? So, and that was another thing. When I got old enough, not a dog I ever owned again would ever die if I could save it." As an adult, Lynda has many pets—dogs, cats, and horses—and these are as important to her as any family member.

Her father's controlling nature during her childhood became oppression in her teen years. Lynda describes feeling caged, trapped, and hopeless. She longed for escape. "Growing up was like prison. Dad was real controlling. I wasn't allowed to date, not even by the time I left home was I allowed to date. He was real strict. So when I left, you know, I left everything. [Her father said,] 'I own you until you're eighteen.' Well, I graduated and left when I was seventeen, not quite eighteen, when I started college." Because her father dominated her life so completely, work for Lynda was a way of having independence and control over herself. She began a forty-hour-a-week job in a nursing home when she was fifteen, saving money for "the day when she could afford to "own herself." When she turned eighteen, things changed dramatically:

> And so I started college in August, so I left and the day I turned 18, I told him, "I'm my own person. Give me my papers. I belong to me now." But yet I wasn't ready for school. And when you're the daughter

of an alcoholic, you tend to do the same things, even though you
didn't like what he did, didn't realize how bad it was, caused problems, and that's what caused the problems. I drank myself right out
of college by spring quarter, and I went to work.

For Lynda, always, work is the answer, the way out of dependence to a
cruel oppressor. And yet throughout this narrative, her story is full of
references to home and to fear of home and dependence on her father's
cruelties. If this job or that experience didn't work out, she would be
"sent home," a sentence to the prison of her childhood dependence on
a tyrant. She states, "You always got an eight-hour notice from me. I
didn't—I couldn't—I was afraid to give a week, because I was afraid
you'd make me not work those two weeks. I was terrified. Couldn't be
out of work. Had to make my own way. Had to do it myself. Couldn't
ask my parents for anything." Work allows Lynda to have selfhood,
identity, and self-reliance. "I was too proud to go back home and ask for
anything. I owned myself. Okay? I just could not do it." Through work
Lynda gained agency and power to resist a dependence on others who
may not be benevolent. "Owning herself" is the ultimate triumph.

Constant Battles

Lynda's repeated fighting—her father, the company, her supervisors, her
co-workers, and even the union—for survival during the first years of
her work at the telephone company are the lines connecting her narrative
to her identity. She fought to prove herself worthy, to make a place for
herself in a "man's" domain, and finally to protect her rights. The tests
that she repeatedly undergoes to prove her worth were both demanding and demeaning, and the men were insistent that she fail and have to
"go home." "We had to do these tests, these dumb tests. I weighed five
pounds [*sic*] then. I had to dead lift a ton of pounds over my head with a
barbell, straight up." She further explains,

> Only if you were going to work with the boys, or outside, that—they
> tried to come up with tests that they could guarantee that the women
> wouldn't kill themselves out there at the pole climbing school. I'm
> not really sure what the tests were for other than that, as a safety net,
> because they'd never had to hire them, and the government comes and
> says "You've got to have women. You've got to have blacks in these
> departments, got to have women in these departments, got to have
> male operators"—because they didn't have those either. Although I

don't know how it can be hard for a man to stay on the phone and say "How can I help you?"

Lynda's home disruption was the primary factor in her need for independence and competence in her work. Repeatedly, she talks of proving herself and of being as "good as the boys." Being competent and capable at work becomes the way that Lynda forestalls poverty, dependence, and the prison of home with her father as jailer.

Hostility toward Homosexuals and Women

At several points during the interview, Lynda expresses hostility toward homosexuals and women, perhaps because of her mother's preference for Lynda's brother, which left her with no ally in her own family, or the brutality she has experienced from men. Perhaps she has grown to identify with her oppressors, shunning the feminine. She spoke off-tape about her brother being "worthless" and "weak." Though he is two years older than she, Lynda is the "strong" one who can be "as good as a man." Later she informed me that all of her family worked at a local telecommunications manufacturing facility, including her brother: "Oh, I have to tell you: just so you understand, my entire family worked for [this company]. My dad retired from there, my mom's brother and his wife, my mom, my brother worked there three times, and got laid off all three times." Her disdain for her brother is evident.

During nine hours of interviews with Lynda, she repeatedly disparaged homosexuals. Once she abruptly demanded to know whether I was "homo or hetero." She had been explaining her dissatisfaction with the union for advocating benefits for same-sex partners of workers, noting that she was adamantly against this change. She also spoke of the weakness of gays and women. Describing a brief stint in the Air Force, she says: "I got over there and—I don't know your sexual preferences, and I don't mean to be prejudiced—I'm hetero. When there's no war on, there's a lot of lesbians in the service. A bunch. And they're closet. That and divorcees. When there's no war going on, and you don't get people you need, you get people that have nothing else to do. And I thought, 'I'm better than that.'" She establishes her identity as different, as heterosexual, perhaps in part because she works in a nontraditional job for women.

Women in particular represent a group that is even harder for Lynda to join than the "boys" in the company. She spoke of being assigned to "light duty" after pregnancy complications. She hated being with the women workers inside. "So [I was put] in the office with a bunch of women who treated me like dirt. If you worked outside with the boys, you'd think the women would be nice to you. [This was] the first time I'd been around women, ever. [There were] ten of them. Lunch time came, they'd go sit in a group, noses up at everybody." She goes on to say that women are the "meanest, ugliest, cruelest bunch. I wouldn't work with women for nothing. Women want to tell the ugliest [gossip]—and you're nobody." Lynda's term of work within the woman-dominated office area was just as traumatic to her as the men had been earlier. "So I was in there a week and I hemorrhaged, and I told them it was because I was in there with them. Told them my baby would have done anything not to be around them." Lynda told me that she believed that if there was a union only of women that had two or more members, that "it wouldn't be nothing but a cat fight."

Initially Lynda expressed support for her sister workers who were vying for men's jobs in the company. They were suffering along with her. However, after describing several years of her career, her narrative reveals her contempt for women who are working at the company, including those who perform outside work as she does. Her disdain for women is apparent. Lynda related her opinions about a woman who had started working at the same time as she had.

> [Cindy] was gorgeous, okay? She was stunningly gorgeous. Blond, blue eyes, skinny, built like a brick house, and had that little southern charm. "Three's Company" was a big show [on television] then. She was a lot like Chrissy on "Three's Company." Blow in that girl's ear on one side and catch the breeze out of the other. Nothing in that brain. And she used that charm to stay with the company. I think they fired her in '88. She managed to hang on about ten years. The men did her work for her.

For Lynda, the other woman's supposed incompetence was even more intolerable since Lynda was trying to prove herself to be as competent as the men. She continued her diatribe against her female co-worker. "See, that just pissed me off. She'd go out and work for somebody, and she'd come in clean and not sweaty, and I'd be out there trying to prove that I could do it, and she'd be like 'Well, I don't know why you get so upset.' I said, 'I get upset because you don't do shit. You know? And I work hard.' And I wasn't ugly then, either, but I didn't want [to be pretty]." Her struggles to find her identity within an environment that is hostile cause her to lash out at everyone, including the women who should have been her compatriots in the battles of work and gender. However, Lynda has effectively isolated herself from women's companionship and solidarity and has also rejected the union while attempting to find a place on her own in the man's world of telecommunications.

In her later years with the company, Lynda remains vehemently anti-union and anti-woman. She has found a space in the man's domain and perhaps has found some peace with age and having fought the battles to get to this point.

> I tried to be one of the boys, and that doesn't work real well either. I don't know really what does work until you get older and they think of you as their mother, 'cause I'm more accepted now than I was then. I was a threat, you know? Either I was too stupid to know anything, or I was too arrogant. I used to tell everybody I have to do twice as much work to be considered half as good. Fortunately, that's not hard to do.

Her tough language reflects the pain and trauma that Lynda has endured, mostly alone, throughout her life. Beginning with her father and her family and continuing in her work life, Lynda has suffered the wounds of patriarchal oppression. Although she has endured years of struggle—at home, in the union, and in the company—Lynda has survived. After twenty-five years of battle, the scars may be healing, but the wounds remain.

[RE]FORMING IDENTITY IN THE MAN'S DOMAIN

For the women in this study who work in male-dominated fields, work becomes a contested site for constructing identity. They forge their identities in the crucibles of resentment, unequal wages, discrimination, and sexual harassment. For many of the women, union membership affords them the democratic process for negotiating power and effecting positive change. While union participation may not be a panacea to the disparities of gender difference at work, many women, including Sally, Suzanne, and Naomi, find that labor unions are the sites for empowerment and transcendence. Unions offer the possibility for women to achieve parity with men in nontraditional roles as they gain access to higher-paying, more autonomous, and more intellectually engaging work. Most of the women in this study who work in the male domain have gained skills and confidence to prove their worth to themselves and others. They have proven that they are as "good as the boys." As greater numbers of women assume leadership—both in the workplace and in the unions—they will enable other women to gain access and equity in the "man's world."

Chapter Four

"I Had to Constantly Fight": Solidarity and Social Activism

For some of the women in this study, union participation and strike activity become the foundations for their social activism and solidarity. In many ways, their stories parallel those of their sisters in labor disputes during the past 150 years in the United States. The collective-subjective and narrative discourse community of these women is situated in their identification with improved labor conditions for their union sisters and brothers. These women's identities are constructed by their service to others in progressive activism. Their language suggests a well-defined identification with fighting for the rights of others—whether on the job, on the picket line, or in their communities. Many of the women in this project devoted their lives to fighting the injustices of the employing class against the working class. The women in this study endeavored to rectify these injustices through social activism that results in union organizing campaigns and strike activity in response to corporate greed. As one respondent reported, "Any company that has a union deserves it." As she and other women noted, unions are necessary whenever workers are threatened or oppressed. One strike veteran and union leader stated that she would never work for her company without union representation.

Many of the women I interviewed spoke of strong unions being necessary to deflect the abuse of economic and position power by their employers. As was true of their sisters in the labor movement in the past, fighting injustice is a powerful motivator for three of the women in this study—Joan, Stella, and Camille. Throughout their narratives, these women spoke of the repeated battles they waged on behalf of workers in their plants, further emphasizing the relentless fight for workers' rights in an environment of job losses and globalization. The increasingly common threats to unions and union workers, as noted in chapter one, are daily obstacles for the women who organize, represent, and lead their union sisters and brothers.

Standing Up for Her Sisters

Historically, workers in North Carolina have alternately resisted and promoted social justice through labor unions. At several important junctures during the past century, organizing efforts by seemingly overpowered workers nevertheless have been successful. One notable example of a woman who made a difference for her fellow workers was Theodosia Gaither Simpson who worked at the R.J. Reynolds Tobacco Company in Winston-Salem. Her story is highlighted in historian Robert Korstad's *Civil Rights Unionism: Tobacco Workers and the Struggle for Democracy in the Mid-Twentieth Century South*. In June 1943, Gaither worked stemming tobacco leaves, a job that was primarily done by women. "African American women, ranging in age from late teens to sixties, performed almost all the stemming in the Reynolds plants."[1] Because of labor shortages during the war, R.J. Reynolds managers forced workers to increase production; in fact, manufacturing vice-president John Whitaker was "aware that his employees were being pushed to work harder than ever before."[2] Simpson was indeed overworked, along with the other women who labored at each of the sixty-five stemming machines in her department. "Each job required dexterity and intense concentration. The room was hot, the work numbingly repetitive, and the dust from the leaf covered everyone from head to foot by the end of the day."[3] The demand for cigarettes during the war caused an intense drive to increase production even though the best and highest paid workers were making only half of what the federal government deemed appropriate to maintain a minimal level of subsistence in a city the size of Winston-Salem at that time. "Few stemmers made more than ten cents above minimum wage, even those who had worked at Reynolds for many years."[4] To make matters worse, Reynolds "manipulated small wage differentials to create divisions among the workers and to encourage dependence on the foreman's goodwill."[5] The increased demands on worker production and the constant monitoring and severe disciplining of the women by the foremen led to even greater dissatisfaction.

Needing "God and a Union"

Nearly desperate, the women in the stemmeries at Reynolds knew that conditions would have to change; they could not keep up the pace and could no longer endure the oppressive conditions in the factory. A union organizing drive began under the auspices of the United Cannery, Agricultural, Packing, and Affiliated Workers of America—Congress

Joan's persistent pursuit of making a difference for others has led her to other important endeavors while she continues to represent the voice of the workers. As she says,

> Here in [my] county I'm involved in a lot of things, and others get very negative about unions. And I said years ago, I said, "You know what? I'm not going to tiptoe around who I am or what I do for a living." So I made the statement to some leaders here in this county, I said, "I work for labor. I'm very proud of what I do, because I make a difference in the lives of people that cannot help themselves. And I'm not going anywhere, so you may as well accept me." And you know what? I don't care where I go, I get support for anything I want here in this county because I don't hide who I am and what I am.

Joan has indeed been an important influence, resulting in positive changes in her union, county, and state. In her career and in her volunteer work, Joan has applied the early lessons of responsibility and care of others to the larger arenas of the work world and community. The members of her union and her fellow citizens have benefited from her labors in the field of social justice.

Joan's current fights for the rights of others echo her earlier efforts as a representative of her local during the 1988 strike at her plant. The original owner of the textile manufacturing facility was, as Joan states, "a good man. I think he was really interested in women being treated fairly and with justice in the plant." However, when his son took over the leadership of the company, Joan says that the younger man told the union representatives in their negotiations: "I'm no longer going to contribute to the retirement fund. I'm no longer going to provide the health insurance premium, and you will not have prescription cards even though you have agreed to a forty-hour work week." Joan notes that the owner's inability to negotiate in good faith with the union led to what she calls an "impasse." In the meeting Joan told him that the membership would be asked to vote on a strike in response to the company's planned cuts. The owner replied that they would not be able to get "people in North Carolina to come out on strike." Joan was appalled by the owner's lack of concern for the workers and his arrogant position that the workers would not strike. Joan states, "It made me so angry because it seemed to me what he was saying to me was that we were too dumb and ignorant to know our rights." She told him that she would go back and report to the membership what had transpired, that nothing had been negotiated. She stated in the meeting: "I will let members make that decision, and we'll see what happens."

When she returned to North Carolina, Joan was burdened with the knowledge that the members would have to face the incontrovertible fact that the "company and the union have come to an impasse." She saw dark days ahead for the workers, but since the company had failed to negotiate in "good faith," the union would have no choice but to fight for their rights. Joan says that she cried when she thought about the hardships that were to come if the workers went out on strike. "And you know, I just thought about my son. My oldest son was getting ready to graduate from high school. And I thought about what all we had gone through all these years with the company. We sacrificed a lot for the company." When she got to the plant, the lead negotiator for the union began to explain the situation to the workers. They did not believe him because, as Joan says, the "company always had someone out there spreading all kinds of rumors and they were bad-mouthing the union." Her colleague had difficulty communicating the extent of the situation to the workers. As she says,

> He had exhausted all means of trying to explain to the workers what had happened. And I said, "Wait a minute." I stood up on a chair, and I told them, I said, "[He] is telling the truth! The company has not bargained with us in good faith after we agreed to the change in the hours, the company said they no longer want to fund the retirement plans; they no longer want to provide our insurance; they no longer want to provide prescription drug cards. And the bottom line is this: they want us to go back to almost minimum wage." And when I said that, they said, "What? We just . . . " And I said, "We got to make a decision. This is not our decision—this is your decision."

Joan's speech affected the workers. Further, she told them: "You have two choices: We can accept the company's proposal, which is nothing. Or we can walk out the door and hit the street." At that point all the workers in the plant began pushing one another to get out of the plant quickly. Joan emphasized that *"everybody in the plant walked out that door. They couldn't get out fast enough."* The plant assistant manager, observing the scene, starting calling out, "'Where y'all going? Where y'all going?'" When Joan told him, "'We are not going to work in this plant if you all are not going to treat us like humans.'" He responded, "'Well that's all right. Get out there. Go on out the door. You'll be back in here tomorrow 'cause it's a hundred and some degrees out there, and I know you're not marching in no heat.'" He, like many other managers before him, underestimated the power of workers when their rights have been violated.

When the workers gathered in the parking lot, the union representative told the group that the membership must take a vote to determine if they would go on strike. In a unanimous vote, the workers agreed to the work stoppage. As Joan marvels, "They cleared the plant. Even people that wasn't in the union came out of the plant with us." The strike committee set up the picket line that hot July, and each worker arrived to walk the picket line every day. To take care of the workers and to organize the strike more carefully, the committee established strike headquarters across the street from the plant. Joan notes that having a strike headquarters close by enabled them "to keep an eye on everything that was going *in* the plant and coming *out* of the plant." When the company hired replacement workers, the striking workers were concerned but resolute. In response, the strike committee established funds to take care of any financial hardships that the workers might face in what would become an eleven-month dispute. As Joan explained, "The committee was in charge of paying hardship funds for house payments, car payments, groceries, whatever." Another important committee was designated to handle all the problems with the strike, and Joan was selected to lead that group as well as to work with the original negotiating committee that periodically was called in to talk with company officials. However, as Joan notes, none of the company's overtures were serious negotiations. The company hired attorneys from a well-known anti-union law firm that included then U.S. Senator Jesse Helms. "They were determined not to negotiate a contract with us, and they were determined that [the striking workers] were never going to go back to work in that plant." Nevertheless, the workers on the picket line were just as determined as the company and their legal team.

As the strike continued into the fall, the workers began to sense that they needed other strategies to force the company to negotiate in good faith with them. They knew that their work consisted of exclusive, intricate lingerie that required highly skilled employees to create quality products. As Joan states, "It had to be done with the utmost quality. We were 100 percent when it comes to quality because the majority of women that went to work there, they *stayed* at that plant." Their solidarity and family-like connections also led to their satisfaction with employment at the plant. Even now, years after the factory closed, workers still gather for a reunion. "Once a year we come together because it was a family. Every baby that was born while we was working at the plant, that was a [plant name] baby. It was just a happy time." The strategy that developed was based on their unique, exclusive garments, so they "started doing things that we thought would make the company recognize that *we* were the best workers that they could ever, *ever* hire." When the replacement workers, predictably, began to produce inferior

garments, the company responded. "The owner started begging us to come
back to work. But we said, 'No, you want us to come back to work, but you
don't want to give us what we want.'" Since the owner would not agree to
their demands, the strikers began to picket the showrooms and corporate
buyers in various states who were considering their company's products.
"We let them know that we were on an unfair labor strike, and the company
wasn't bargaining in good faith with us." The workers even went to stores
where the lingerie was sold. "We went to those stores and we handed out
flyers and we told them our story." Though these tactics eventually had an
effect on the company, the owner responded by subcontracting work out to
other companies. The striking workers found out about it through examining
the company's trash, thereby staying ahead of them, "knowing every step
that they were making." They then picketed the company's subcontractors.

Joan's fight for justice led her to confront managers at the subcontracting plants, a task that was difficult and stressful initially. When Joan spoke
with the managers and explained the reasons for the strike, the subcontractors, "threw the work out. They were very nice." The only group of people
who were not open to the strikers, other than company officials, was the
replacement workers. Joan states that they "were *real* nasty." The replacement workers were filled with propaganda about the company's conflict with
the workers. As Joan recalls,

> We was walking on the strike line and walking *every day* except for on
> Sunday. When they would work on Saturday, they would go to work at
> six o'clock, and in the fall and winter, it was real dark in the morning.
> And we would be out there on the strike line walking in the *dark*. They
> would be saying different things to us, like, "You need to go home!"
> Sometimes it was very nerve-wracking. It was a tough strike because I
> was very much a leader in the strike, and in fact, I had my life threat-
> ened several times.

Joan recounts the potentially violent incidents while walking the picket line.
"The workers that crossed the strike line, their [relatives] would bring them
up, and they would try and run us down [with their cars]." When a car
nearly hit striking workers one morning, Joan filed a report at the police
station, which led to increased support by the police with additional patrol-
ling of the picket line and strike headquarters.

"Some Determined Women"

The "tough strike" was made even more difficult by its duration. Over time,
the women who were walking the picket line grew weary of the constant

stress. "It lasted so long that it got to the place that it was working on some of the workers' nerves, but they never would give up. They would never give up because you got to understand, we went on strike in July, spent Thanksgiving on the strike line, and come Christmas, then we walked in the *snow*." The union was supportive, and the women were persistent. "I would say that we were some determined women. We did not give up. I mean those women out there really had pride in what they were doing." Because of the threats to their rights, the workers fought the company, holding firm to their convictions. Joan was right by their side through the worst of it, counseling and leading the workers in solidarity with the faith that they would win this fight for workers' justice. She said that the workers had an unshakeable resolve to retain their due benefits.

> And they had took pride in themselves and they had worked for that company all those years, and they said that they wasn't giving up. The main issue was their retirement. If we hadn't stayed on strike and *went* on strike, there would be many women right now that would *not* have drawn their retirement. Because [the company] was not going to fund the retirement any more. And that means that the retirement benefit would have been cut by at least 50 percent.

Their efforts were well paid at least in the short term when the company finally had lost so much money that the owner began to negotiate in earnest with the union leaders in an official capacity. "We got everything back we had lost. That's the first strike [in North Carolina] that we ever had where we won the strike and won full, full benefits that we had prior to the strike."

The workers' triumph was complete; however, Joan sustained losses from the toll that the strike, the picketing, and the negotiations had taken on her personal life. She said that she was the last person to return to work in the plant when the strike concluded. "I was the last one to go back to work. I was real bitter because the company had did so many things to me." A number of events led to Joan's bitterness toward the company. When a union member died during the strike, the striker's bereaved son was directed by the company to seek out Joan on the picket line, blaming her for the loss of funds. The man showed up with a gun and said he was going to kill her for preventing him from getting his mother's death benefits. "He had a *gun*, and he was going to *kill* me that day. And then my business agent jumped in front of me, and he *grabbed* [the son], and he grabbed the gun. And he got back in the car. I'll never forget it. That was something else upsetting." Joan's bitterness stemmed from the company's insistence that she was the cause of the strike, the instigator and leader of the dispute. "I was so bitter because they turned everything on *me*. It was a tough strike on me. A lot of things happened to *me*, a lot of the workers don't even know. I took the heat for them, you know. And I had to stay strong in order for them to be strong." She nearly decided not to go back into the plant, but she changed her mind when she reflected on the women workers who had fought alongside her. "I went back because I am devoted to the membership." When her business agent, noting her distress, offered her a position in the union, she said, "No, I'm not going to let them beat me. And I didn't want to work for the union." However, when she returned to work, the pressure was relentless. "I went back, but they treat me so *bad*. And they would have started taking money from [the workers], cheating them out of their money. I had to fight for them all the time. I had to fight, to constantly fight with the company. *All* the time." Her efforts on behalf of the workers seemed endless.

Joan's business agent finally convinced Joan that the best way to protect the workers would be as a union representative though this decision was difficult for her. On her final day as an employee, Joan told the manager, "'I'm through fighting. I've devoted my life to this company, and it seems like you want to take everything away from me.' I left there that day in tears and came home. And I'll never forget, I came to the phone, and I called [my representative] and said, 'I'm ready.'" When the regional representative later hired her, Joan took a week off to consider her new position. She went back to the plant as the business agent, and the manager had to answer to her in negotiations and other union-worker matters. Though the striking workers had been successful in working for their rights and for fair negotiations, the company closed the plant a mere four years later, a union-busting tactic that continues to plague manufacturing workers in North Carolina more than a decade later. Joan still works for the union, continuing her fight against injustice.

> I still struggle and try and help workers, resolving problems with the company, and just working to insure that workers are treated with justice on the job and fairness. Because in North Carolina, unless you are represented by a union, you are at the mercy of the employer. [Though] I try to be fair with both parties, I'm not going to allow an employer to treat a worker less than a human without any justice. Because our feelings are all we have. And I always say that a worker cannot produce their best if they're working under stress.

She fights for others because of her great sense of dedication and responsibility to others, for as she says, "I believe that if there's any way that I can help *anybody* I'm always out there. I believe that if you have lived your life and not have made some difference in someone else's life, it's all been in vain." Clearly Joan continues to make a powerful difference in the fight for justice.

ELIZABETH GURLEY FLYNN AND ONE BIG UNION

In another era, in another state, Elizabeth Gurley Flynn stood at the cusp of change as women workers fought injustices in their workplaces. From 1906 to 1917, Flynn was involved with the Industrial Workers of the World (IWW), the so-called "One Big Union," which had formed in 1905 to "end the use of workers against each other anywhere—in the same plant, or in the same industry, or across oceans, in peace or in war, either to cut each other's pay or kill each other's kids."[9] In 1912 in Lawrence, Massachusetts, Flynn and other IWW organizers attempted to assist more than 20,000 woolen and cotton mill workers who went out on strike. According to Baxandall and Gordon, Flynn was moved by the plight of the poor workers, primarily immigrants from at least twenty-five different countries, and she sought ways to guide and support them. She was appalled by the meager pay and the oppressive conditions of the workers in the Lawrence mills.

> Wages were already at the starvation point. The highest paid weavers received $10.50 weekly. Spinners, carders, spoolers and others averaged $6 to $7 weekly. Whole families worked in the mills to eke out a bare existence. Pregnant women worked at the machines until a few hours before their babies were born. Sometimes a baby came right there in the mill, between the looms. The small pittance taken from the workers by the rich corporations, which were protected by a high tariff from foreign competition, was the spark that ignited the general strike. "Better to starve fighting than to starve working!" became their battle cry.[10]

Flynn reported on the many atrocities enacted against the workers and their families during the strike, including an organized police state that precipitated a violent attack on the striking workers by more than 1400 members of the state militia. In the melee, a woman striker, Anna LaPizza, was killed. During meetings with the workers and their families, Flynn and Bill Haywood, the leader of the IWW, talked about the power of a united union of the working people against the wealthy and powerful owners.

> We spoke of their power, as workers, as the producers of all wealth, as the creators of profit. Here they could see it in Lawrence. Down tools,

fold arms, stop the machinery, and production is dead—profits no longer flow. We ridiculed the police and militia in this situation. "Can they
weave cloth with soldiers' bayonets or policemen's clubs?" we asked.
"No," replied the confident workers. "Did they dig coal with bayonets
in the miners' strikes or make steel or run trains with bayonets?" Again
the crowds roared, "No." We talked Marxism as we understood it—
the class struggle, the exploitation of labor, the use of state and armed
forces of government against the workers. It was all there in Lawrence
before your eyes.[11]

The strike was ultimately responsible for wage increases of up to 7.5 percent
in the woolen mills and from five to seven percent in the cotton mills. Flynn's
assistance in the fight for worker justice had positive outcomes.

Social Conscience and Activism

Meanwhile, Flynn was shaping a social conscience that had begun when she
joined the IWW as a teenager. Her involvement in the IWW would eventually lead her to become a founding member of the American Civil Liberties
Union.[12] "In 1907 Flynn became a full-time organizer for the IWW, traveling
all over the Eastern U.S. to join garment and restaurant labor struggles, to
assist with a miners strike in Minnesota, and to support a lumber strike in
Montana. She would be arrested numerous times as an agitator in some of
the major labor struggles of the period . . . "[13] Her life and work with the
IWW and for women's rights, free speech, and civil liberties reflect her chief
purpose: fighting injustice.

A professed Marxist, Flynn saw capitalism and greedy owners as the
sources of injustice and endeavored to raise consciousness about these issues.
She once stated, "I despise the rule of Rockefeller and Morgan as much as
that of King or Kaiser."[14] At a May Day speech in 1939, Flynn compared
socialist ideas to her experiences in the South. "In 1914 I spent May Day in
the far South, speaking in a Tampa, Fla, public park. Spanish, Cuban, Mexican cigarmakers were there; many natives too. They were familiar with the
textile strikes and expressed great sympathy for the victims of 'Yankee greed.'
Little did we realize how soon the textile barons would run away South and
precipitate similar bloody conflicts not so far away."[15] Flynn's activism had
a significant impact on the lives of workers. As Mary Heaton Vorse reported
in her reminiscences about the Lawrence Strike, Flynn was able to inspire the
strikers to continue on their difficult path.

> When Elizabeth Gurley Flynn spoke, the excitement of the crowd
> became a visible thing. . . . She stirred them, lifted them up in her

appeal for solidarity. Then at the end of the meeting, they sang. It was as though a spurt of flame had gone through this audience, something stirring and powerful, a feeling which has made the liberation of people possible; something beautiful and strong had swept through the people and welded them together, singing.[16]

In reality, Flynn and the other IWW organizers had the vision and the spirit to fight injustice while offering something better, "One Big Union of All the Workers." In her elder years, Flynn remained passionate about the value of unions. In a speech delivered in 1962 when she was seventy-two years old, she reminded her audience that health insurance, pensions, and paid vacations were the result of union efforts to improve the workers' lot. "All of these things have come into existence since the period of the IWW."[17] She further noted that even more important than worker wages was the increased production demand of automation. "We never thought of such a thing that there would be a decreased labor force and increased production and that part of the plant would be left idle and the other part would produce more than the whole plant at one time."[18] In her long career as an activist, Flynn had been at the forefront of resistance to corporate control over the conditions of labor. Her fiery spirit lives on in the women unionists who are organizing and building union strength.

STELLA: THE "BIG ME-LITTLE YOU" CONCEPT

Stella is a contemporary North Carolina woman unionist fighting for justice. Like Elizabeth Gurley Flynn, Stella views life in her small mountain community in an analytical framework that includes questioning authority and resisting the status quo. A natural philosopher and a keen observer, Stella comments on the many injustices that have been perpetrated against poor and working-class people throughout the history of western North Carolina. When I first called her to arrange an interview, she immediately began recounting her work and family histories, the stories spilling out as we talked on the telephone. She said, "My parents were growing up here, and this was a very poor county. They couldn't afford to buy a home. All they had was money for groceries. With four children to feed, there was nothing left. My father worked in the tanneries. This county's only industries were pulpwood and the tanneries before [the paper mill came]." Stella indicated that the poverty that her parents endured was caused by unorganized workers looking out "for number one." Further, she notes, "'My grandfather worked at the Carr Lumber Company where they gave the workers just enough money to live on. This also was a result of not having a union." Stella recounted her family's experiences with wealthy and powerful men and women who have what she calls the "Big Me-Little-You" concept "that rich people have." One of the most dramatic examples of her idea occurred late in the nineteenth century. "George Vanderbilt [the railroad baron] stole one hundred acres that my grandfather had bought for thirty dollars in the Pisgah Forest up near the Pink Beds. He's another one of those rich bastards who made money off the poor people." The series of unfair and oppressive actions taken against the working people of her community led Stella to become an active unionist.

Stella has lived her entire life within the confines of her small mountain county, and she worked forty-nine years for the paper company that was the economic mainstay of the community. Prior to the arrival of the company in 1939, as Stella states, the community was dependent on pulpwood and tanneries, which added to the wealth of the very few individual families who owned them while keeping the workers and their families in poverty. She notes, "See, that's what happens when you got an economy where it's 'Big Me and Little You.' 'Cause they're going to keep you that way. If they ever get you like that, they're going to keep you there. So that's why it is so important to have unions." The paper mill thrived for decades, led by a benevolent owner who believed in the workers' well-being, paying them sustainable wages and providing other services and incentives as part of a welfare capitalist program. For example, the owner established the county's first health care facility, an on-site infirmary, and provided recreational facilities and sports teams. In addition, Stella notes with pride, the owner supported the schools and offered music lessons, band uniforms, and instruments for the children. Stella herself was a band member. At the height of the company's success under the founder's leadership, the workers enjoyed a higher standard of living, better pay, and stronger community ties. "My mother worked outside the home when most children's mothers did not. We grew up in rented homes because [my family] couldn't afford to buy a house." After the paper mill was built and better paying jobs were to be found, individuals' prosperity increased. Stella and her siblings all bought homes of their own. Their economic status was not to last, however. When a major corporation bought the plant, the company sold the recreational facilities and cut costs to boost their profits. When these cuts began affecting the workers pay and benefits, a union was formed to help retain workers' rights and benefits.

We Shall Not Be Moved

Stella became a fervent union supporter, learning more about how the union could fight injustice during two major strikes. She learned that workers' solidarity could combat the oppression of the rich and the powerful. The first strike lasted eight weeks, and Stella indicated that she gained important knowledge about the power of unions during that time. "It helped me an *awful lot*, the strike. It helped me to see that there were times in a person's life where it was more important to stand together than to be selfish. *Everybody* helped *everybody* [during the strike]. There was groceries just piled at the union hall." After the dispute with the company was settled, Stella was convinced that unions were the workers' only power. She says, "I one hundred per cent believe in the unions. And if anybody has got any knowledge at all of the economy and what goes on with the money market and all that, if they got any knowledge at all, they know that their salary was based on, even though they're not in the union, their salary is based on what union people make." She further notes that the current conditions for workers in the county, state, and nation are indicative of the unions' loss of power. "Or course, it's going back [to the pre-union conditions] now. People are going to get to where they were when they couldn't afford to buy a house. [Many people] can't afford to buy houses now."

The company and the union engaged in a final labor dispute in 2001 when an international businessman bought the company and began efforts to slash workers' pay—up to 60 percent in some cases—and to cut all workers' benefits. When the union leaders and the membership decided to strike, the company did not offer to negotiate. The new owner simply informed the workers that he would shut down the plant and sell it rather than concede to honor their current agreement about working conditions, pay, and benefits. At this time Stella determined that she would speak up on behalf of the union and the injustices that faced the workers. She said that "most of the people in this town hate the union." When I asked her why that was so, Stella indicated that they blamed the union for the job losses and the eventual loss of the major employer in the county. She said that they did this out of what she called, "*total, unadulterated ignorance.*" She further stated that the people in town "have no idea. They're working up there, probably three dollars an hour and they don't think that people ought to make any more than that. That's the stupid part." Stella has an in-depth understanding of the economics of the situation, a knowledge that seems to come from her long years of watching and listening to the "Big Me's" of the world trying to take advantage of the relative weakness of individual workers and poor people. She notes that the workers did not organize the union until the company no longer supported workers' rights although the company was, as she put it, "booming." Their "obscene" profits when juxtaposed with the workers' comparatively paltry compensation sparked the union organization effort. "Other companies, [our] customers, were unionized. And I can remember in the 1970s that we supplied three-fourths of the world with cigarette paper. And we'd go to factories and we had the market [cornered] because of our quality. Fine paper was a very complicated process. And we constantly did research to make it better." At that time, the company had been taken over by six local men, all of whom had one objective: to get rich and get out. Therefore the philosophy and management style became focused only on profits. As several women, including Stella, reported, the paper mill owners became millionaires at the expense of the workers and the company.

Developing a Sense of Justice

Though Stella learned how to be a fighter for workers' rights by observing the experiences of her family and fellow workers, several incidents in her mother's life also contributed to her sense of justice. Early in life, Stella's mother performed in a musical group, and rich families would hire the band to play for their parties. However, these families paid the musicians not in cash, but in fruit. The poor members of the band would accept the meager offerings from their wealthy customers, simply because there was little else that they could do, just as whenever they needed to travel, even great distances, they walked. When her mother and her friends were walking and met rich people traveling in their cars, Stella's mother would "speak," or wave to them in greeting. When she did this, Stella's mother reported that the passengers would laugh at her and tell her that she had "the nerve to speak to them." Though this was degrading, Stella noted that her mother was a "feisty woman" who later operated a saloon to help raise her family. Later on when the family was more prosperous, and the children were grown, Stella's mother managed to buy a house of her own and to purchase a rental house as well.

When the local river, polluted with the paper mill dyes and processing fluids, contaminated the wells on her mother's properties, Stella's mother asked for her children's advice. Since both Stella and her brother worked for the company, her mother asked them if this conflict with their employer would affect their jobs. They told their mother that she should pursue the complaint without regard for their jobs. Both company officials and a town lawyer laughed at Stella's mother when she said that the paper mill would have to pay for the loss of her property and rental income. Her mother finally went to a lawyer in a neighboring county who read the fine print of the sales contract of the mill, which required the company to pay for damages downstream. All he had to do was write a letter to the company, and they settled out of court. The company bought her mother's property for a fair price and found her another place to live.

So this "feisty woman" fought the big company and won. "She went to great lengths to find out [what to do about the situation]." Stella says that her mother "went after it. And won. And other people had lost and just went their way. But not my mother. I learned [my determination] from her."

Though her early dream of becoming a surgeon was not fulfilled because of time and circumstance, Stella became adept at working for the benefit of others. She worked as a temporary supervisor for seven years with more than one hundred people in a department. When she made her rounds throughout the plant with a bad hip, Stella endured the pain for the sake of others. "I was walking so much. You got one hundred people to help look out after, and you're on the go constantly. And I was. There was people that would just go to another department and hide or sit around and not help. But I was always there." Stella's work also caused her to sacrifice her personal life in many ways. Her dedication to the workers jeopardized her marriage. She wed at age thirty, but the marriage was short-lived. She explains the situation with a sigh,

> Of course, it didn't work out. And life continued on. You know. He wanted me to quit work and he wanted me to go to Atlanta with him. And I should have. Yeah, I should have. Because my job and the people I worked with were all I really cared about. I didn't care that much about him. But I should have. And if I hadn't been the type of person that I am with the drive that I had to work—work was everything. I could've given up lots of stuff and been a housewife. Of course, I never had any kids. And I wish I'd had kids. But I worked those shifts.

Stella's commitment to worker justice and to improving life for others comprised her life during forty-nine years at the paper mill. Her additional significant contribution to others occurred when members of her family fell ill and needed her care. First, her brother died of a brain tumor. In response to his death, her mother later took an overdose of medication, had a stroke, and was bedridden. Stella took care of her until her mother's death two years later. And two years after her mother's death, her father became ill and died suddenly. These losses have taken a toll on Stella's life though her spirit is bright and indomitable. She remains a pro-union activist, stating that the "stupid people against unions just help rich people drain poor people of their life." Her fights for worker justice and her care and concern for family members—for the "Little You's" of the world—ultimately tell the story of one woman activist who gave of herself that others might benefit.

LEONORA BARRY: PROFESSIONAL LABOR ORGANIZER

The ideology and activism of Stella and Elizabeth Gurley Flynn echoes that of their predecessor, Leonora Barry, a hosiery worker who was the first woman to be a professional labor organizer. In 1886, as a member of the Knights of Labor, Barry became a staunch supporter of women's participation in unions. A widow with two children, Barry initially began working in a factory to support her family. After years of service, she later worked closely with the Knights to assemble nearly one thousand women at a union-organizing rally. She "traveled extensively for the Knights, organizing women's and men's locals, lecturing on women's issues, and lobbying for protective labor legislation."[19] Her fight against injustice was tremendously successful since she "established not only union locals but also some cooperative factories and a working women's benefit fund."[20] The source of Barry's activism originated with her own life, but her work with the Knights of Labor enabled her to see the important role that unions have in improving the lives of working people, particularly women workers. The Knights were an open and inclusive organization, involving women and people of color by 1881, and organizing as many as "50,000 women into local units;" however, as Barry was to learn later, women workers benefited from having a separate organization to serve their special needs.[21] Barry's field reports from four years of traveling and observing working conditions in factories did much to bring about needed change for industrial workers.

Although Barry recorded the owners' unkindness and animosity toward workers, she also noted that workers often acted out of self-interest and factionalism rather than acting in accordance with the good of the whole. The mill owners that Barry investigated were successful capitalists who would exploit workers—most of whom were women—for increased profits. Within the Knights of Labor, Barry exhorted the men to support pay equity demands, without which, she noted, "our platform has been but a mockery of the principles intended."[22] The long hours, low wages, and intolerable working conditions were especially oppressive to working women, so Barry was amazed to find that one of the worst owners was a woman.

> Not among male employers alone in this city, but a woman in whose heart we would expect to find a little pity and compassion for the suffering of her own sex. To the contrary, on this occasion, however, I found one, who for cruelty and harshness toward employees, has not an equal on the pages of labor's history—one who owns [a women's

and children's garment factory]. Upon accepting a position in her factory an employee is compelled to purchase a sewing machine from the
proprietress . . . . This must be paid for in weekly payments of 50
cents, provided the operative makes $3. Should she make $4 the weekly
payment is 75 cents.[23]

The worker would "forfeit the machine" if some "petty tyrannical rule"
was broken, for example, illness, anger, or leaving the job. The forfeited
sewing machine was resold to the next victim. Moreover, the deplorable
conditions of this factory included forcing the workers to buy their own
thread, leaving them with $2.50 at most per week to live on.[24]

Segregated Unions for Women

Barry was a tireless organizer and educator, having spent the majority of
her career working for the rights of others. Her pursuit of justice for workers was founded, like Stella's, in a philosophy that suggested that greed
and ignorance were responsible for the abysmal plight of workers. She said
that "slop shops" [sweat shops] were reprehensible in a civilized society,
with "garments manufactured by men who sacrifice human happiness, life
and immortal souls on the altar of selfish greed and low, sordid, groveling
ambition."[25] Barry later saw that endeavors that separated working wom-
en's issues from men's were futile. While talking and working alongside
women who were involved in trade unions, Barry noted that women often
faced obstacles in male-dominated unions; nevertheless she insisted that
men and women work together in desegregated unions. "Although Barry
found women workers to be happier in separate locals, she herself believed
this to be a mistaken approach and ended her organizing career recom-
mending that the Knights' separate Woman's Department be abolished."[26]
She urged the leaders of the Knights of Labor to integrate the union while
encouraging more women to teach their union and non-union sisters the
economic lessons of industrial production about which they were ignorant.
Ultimately, however, Leonora Barry proclaimed that women's place was in
the home whenever financially possible and that men should be the provid-
ers of the family. This statement preceded her marriage to another Knight,
whereupon Barry quit her position as union organizer "although she was
to remain a political activist and public speaker until her death in 1930."[27]
Barry ultimately contributed to improvement of conditions and the empowerment of workers during her career with the Knights, but she turned to a
more traditional standpoint when her personal circumstances changed. She
had viewed both perspectives in the labor issue for women and had moved
away from the inchoate feminist consciousness that she and her working

sisters had begun to develop. When Barry married again, she ceased all of her union activities.

CAMILLE: CHRISTIAN ACTIVIST FOR WORKERS

While her union sisters may have taken a Marxist view of workers' lives and conditions, another paper mill worker, Camille, exemplifies a Christian viewpoint that encompasses both family and the union. Her search for justice for workers—union and non-union—stem from her involvement with the PACE international union as well as her work as a non-union employee during her thirty-eight years with the company. She recounts her experiences in 1971 when the union was formed. "I, at the time, helped organize the union, or helped get it together." As one of the primary local organizers, Camille took the union representatives to visit in the homes of workers. She introduced the ideas of worker justice to her fellow employees, some of whom were rude to the organizers. When they later became members and staunch supporters, Camille wondered at the change in the workers' attitudes. Organizing efforts were fruitless at the beginning, a fact that Camille attributed to older workers who were complacent at first. "But at the time we felt like that we did need a union. I don't know how many times it was voted on. But the main thing that always kept the union out was the older people." However, later in the organizing efforts, the older people began to notice how the company was replacing older workers with younger people. "The company started mistreating the older people, started getting rid of them, that kind of thing." The next union election was successful. "Then [the older workers realized that they] really didn't have that security. So the *old* ones decided *they* needed a union too. And when it was voted on the *next* time it did come in." The successful union organizing drive was the beginning of Camille's worker justice campaign, and while she was never, as she says, "an officer in the union," she was nonetheless an important leader who spoke up for the rights of workers.

Camille worked in the finishing department for eleven years, until the plant began to institute rotating eight-hour shifts, and she was unable to spend time with her husband. After working for years with a group of people who were a family in her department, Camille made the difficult decision to look for "day work" to be able to spend time with her spouse. "When I first started work down there, we just worked five days. When you worked shifts you had days, evening, and graveyard." This decision involved even more conflict since Camille was an avid union member, and seeking a job in the office meant that she would now be a non-union employee. In addition, the difference in pay was dramatic. She says, "I went ahead and got a day job. I had to take such a big cut to come to days. 'Cause your money's in shifts. But you got to work nights, graveyards, and weekends. But to get on days, I went ahead and took the cut to work days, up until the plant shut down and all the layoffs." The loss of pay was astonishing to Camille. As she says, "You have to work shifts, and you have to do physical labor. Which I understand that, but there shouldn't have been that much of a difference in pay." This new situation brought Camille to yet another opportunity to raise concerns about pay equity and worker justice in office jobs as well. She notes that the work in the office is both demanding and relentless.

> Because [when] you work in the office, just mentally you worked just as hard as you worked down there [in the plant]. And of course you're home at night and on the weekend. But still it's like when you work shifts [in the plants] and you work a shift and somebody comes in and takes over. Where when you work in the office, it's laying there waiting on you. So that would be one thing about all this stuff that really doesn't seem fair because we're all contributing towards the same goal.

Camille's unique perspective shows both sides of the issue of union and non-union employees. "I've been on both sides. It takes all of us working together."

The Other Side

Eventually, the worst difficulty that Camille faced was with her fellow workers, those for whom she had labored to improve working conditions and salary throughout the years. However, when she was a union employee during the strike, Camille was shaken to learn that the non-union employees had such anger and hatred toward the striking workers. She says, "That could be awfully discouraging sometimes to think about how people felt about the strike and the workers." Years later, when she was on the "other side of the fence" and had to cross the picket line as a salaried office employee, Camille was again amazed at the bitter recriminations that striking workers hurled at those crossing the line. She could see "both sides." She further explains, "As far as union and non-union, I've been on both sides of that, too. So I try to look at both sides, but it's sad when you have such animosity between people that I had to face when I had to cross the picket line at my job. I had no choice. And being yelled at and all this, that, and the other where it's just supposed to be people you know." Always concerned about the rights of the workers on either side of the picket line, Camille understands the needs of both parties to do their work.

> When I was in the union, I walked the picket line. To me, the [non-union workers] were in the office and salaried, they had to go in there. That's their job. [When I was a salaried employee], I had to go in there. [During the earlier strike] I had a right to stand out there and picket. And they had a right to go in. Just the same way, this last time, they [union workers] had a right to stand out there and picket, and I had a right to go in. It was my job.

Eventually Camille focuses this emotional and personal issue on individual rights and the just actions of employees on both sides of the conflict. She notes, "It's like one group says, 'I have all the rights and you have no rights.'" Through all the difficulties, however, Camille remains a staunch union supporter. She stated, "I'm still pro-union."

Working "As Unto the Lord"

Her pro-union position enables Camille to empathize with union workers with whom she no longer shares common interests and to speak up for their rights even when it is difficult to do so. After she had been employed in the office a number of years, an administrator found a list of union organizers with Camille's name on it, and he confronted her. "They had a list of people that helped organize the union. My name was on that list. And I laughed and said, 'Well, it's the company's own fault.' I think any time a union goes in, it's the company's fault. If they had treated people right and done right, there would never have been a union." Camille's belief in unions and her fight for worker justice often placed her in conflict with members of her church family. When asked why she sided with the strikers, Camille commented that it was her Christian duty to support the downtrodden. "I'm one of these too, I believe that everybody's got their rights on the picket line. I told 'em at church I said that I felt like as a Christian; you work as unto the Lord. It was my responsibility. I had a job. And responsibility to my job. And if they told me to come in, that was my responsibility to the Lord." Her Christian faith extends into the difficulties that she and other workers have faced since the plant was closed. She says that she "has had a job all that time and the Lord has blessed me for so many years." She also notes that many workers are in worse shape from the tragic closing of the plant that had been a mainstay of the community for sixty-two years. "Lots of people, including me, have been raised on [the paper mill]." This fact makes the loss of work and the loss of benefits even more devastating. Camille stated that the "plant shutdown affects *everybody*. But different people in different ways. Some people, both husband and wife worked there. Some of them's got kids in college. I think it is sad that the doors are shut." She blames the powerful and the rich for the loss. "Nothing's like it used to be anymore. Companies used to take care of [the workers]. Where now it's business profits, the bottom line is profit. And [the worker] is just a nothing." Like Joan and Stella, Camille understands that the "Big Me" is likely to win in the unfair economic battles between workers and owners.

SOCIAL ACTIVISM FOR CHANGE

The women in this study, like their union sisters in the past, have learned powerful lessons from their union and strike experiences. They will fight for the underdog, the downtrodden, and the powerless through any means available to them, whether through organizing a union local, speaking up for others and educating the public, or engaging in union activism. However, just as Stella's mother and others have learned, "feisty women" can effect lasting social change for workers. At times, as in Joan's case, they may influence the empowerment of workers by speaking up for people in the working class. Otherwise, as did Camille, they may involve the workers in effecting their own transformation and empowerment by engaging in union organizing activities or by marching on the picket lines. Social activism through labor unions for the women in this study emerges as a powerful tool to fight oppression of the workers by wealthy owners. The "Big Me" people may be opposed by an organized challenge on their absolute power and authority. The women in this study have learned that the social activism of labor unions enabled them to claim agency and power. As their foremothers—Theodosia Simpson, Elizabeth Gurley Flynn, and Leonora Barry—demonstrated, together workers can institute a democratic workplace, thereby ensuring access to fair employment, just compensation, and humane working conditions.

Chapter Five

"I Just Couldn't Say No": Self-Abnegation and Sacrifice

Patriarchy and economic oppression figure prominently in the lived experiences of southern working-class women who often subscribe—consciously or not—to an ethics of care. Caring is a positive feminine response posed by Nell Noddings and Carol Gilligan that may lead to selfless sacrifice at its best and martyrdom at its worst—within an oppressive, patriarchal system. Ella May Wiggins and Crystal Lee Jordan are two well-known working-class women in North Carolina who have been martyrs for labor unions. The experiences of these women parallel those of women in this study. The self-abnegation that Wiggins, Jordan, and other working-class women often experience has been previously documented. Throughout the history of labor disputes in the United States, many women have sacrificed to improve conditions of others—whether for individuals in their personal spheres or in the collective lot of workers in their communities. Many times working-class women are faced with extreme choices and challenges, situations where they give all they have—even their lives—to the cause and for other people. Three women in this study, Rose, Katherine, and Annie, have sacrificed important aspects of their lives in both personal and public domains in order to nurture and support others. Their ethics of care in relationships and in the broader scheme of the work world depend on sacrifice and denial of self. Ultimately these women's losses prove to be gains for those who are cared for in their lives. At times the sacrifices of these women amount to nothing less than martyrdom.

Theories of Caring

The theories behind women's self-effacement and loss are many, but the work of Nell Noddings and Carol Gilligan focus on the caring work of women in relation to others and within institutions. According to Nell Noddings, men have been taught to emulate the fiercest warriors or the most pious and long-suffering monks, ultimately becoming extremists in order to win the battles of their choosing. Noddings' relational ethics of caring allows for a different viewpoint, one espoused by women. Rosemary Tong in *Feminine and Feminist Ethics*, suggests that Noddings' viewpoint is problematic since it places women in the role of martyr. Tong states, "Must victims become martyrs, seeking relation over and over when all they receive in return is abuse?"[1] In a patriarchal society, it is dangerous for women to be self-effacing and forgiving, paving the way for greater domination and oppression. The inequalities inherent in Noddings' relational ethics of care "leaves open the risk of abuse."[2] Tong notes that "insofar as unequal relationships are unequal, they may become paradigms for domination-submission."[3] Herein lies the problem with the relational ethics of care. "Unless I expect from my intimate what I demand from myself, and unless what I demand from myself is what my intimate expects from me, our relationship cannot be an entirely morally good one. Certainly it cannot be an equal one."[4] Moreover, the problem of self-effacement is exacerbated by the ethics of care urging women to think of others' needs to the exclusion of their own. "A unidirectional mode of caring does little to teach the cared-for about the burdens of the one-caring, and it does even less to teach the one-caring about the legitimacy of her own needs and wants."[5] Noddings' ethics of care has also been criticized for reifying the idea of self-sacrifice, often a detriment to women in particular. As Tong asserts, a "self disconnected from others may be a solipsistic atom, but a self totally welded to others is no longer a self."[6] Self-sacrifice, then, becomes an ideal that leads to further loss and oppression.

In a similar fashion, Carol Gilligan extols the virtues of caring and concern for others. She highlights the apparent dichotomy between men's and women's responses to the world. Women, she says, "tend to espouse an ethics of care that stresses relationships and responsibilities, whereas men tend to espouse an ethics of justice that stresses rules and rights."[7] In reviewing women's moral development stages, Gilligan notes that women at level one are insecure and dependent, intent only on pain avoidance and survival. However, in level two, women are willing to reach out to others, often denying their own needs. "In many ways, the Level Two woman is the conventional, nurturant woman who equates goodness with self-sacrifice and who tries to subjugate her wants to those of other people. In extreme cases, such a woman comes to believe that it is *always* 'selfish' for her to do what she wants."[8] As Gilligan points out, these women necessarily reach a destructive point, or either they learn to take care of themselves while ministering to others' needs. One of the criticisms of Gilligan's moral development stages is that level two operates to forestall the loneliness of level one, but that level two is also a strategy for negotiating the male-dominated world. "Although Level Two is frequently described as altruistic, as if women always *freely* choose to put other people's needs and interests ahead of their own, in reality Level Two is simply another coping mechanism. Within a patriarchy, women learn that men will reward, or at least not punish, the women who faithfully serve them."[9] Finally, as Tong suggests, care may be an element in relations between men and women as long as the care is given *freely*, "and the one caring is not taken for granted. As long as men *demand* and *expect* caring from women, both sexes will morally shrink: Neither men nor women will be able to authentically care."[10]

Similarly, Eleanora Patterson, in "Suffering," notes that women's suffering for the sake of others is a "misalignment," with men taking "little caretaking responsibility for others individually or on a social scale."[11] Suffering then is not the path to a more enlightened society, but one that leads a person to a "deeply powerful" experience. The Civil Rights movement was the impetus of Patterson's deepening understanding about the martyred role that many women assume in the world. Rather than suffering passively and piously, women and other oppressed groups could engage in protest and advocate for their collective rights. "I felt an exhilarating sense of connection with others in standing up for more hopeful and respectful ways of living together."[12] Her work with others in solidarity limited her suffering and kept her from becoming a martyr. Working together gave the workers power. When a woman works alone, subverting herself and denying her own rights to self-development and agency, she becomes a victim, a martyr for others. As Patterson and others have shown, collective action is the antidote to individual martyrdom. Collective action through labor unions provides working-class women with the means to avoid self-sacrifice in the public domain. The women in this study, as did their union sisters before them, demonstrate the problems of self-abnegation and sacrifice.

ROSE: HAVING NO "AMBITION"

Rose, a former paper worker from the North Carolina mountains, is one of the martyrs in this study. At age eighty-two, Rose is perhaps the most self-effacing and downtrodden of all the women I interviewed. Throughout three hours of interviews on two occasions, Rose repeatedly questioned the value of her experiences, both in the mill and in her personal life, though she has subsumed all of her own desires in the service of others. She never married, instead taking care of her elderly parents and providing for two younger sisters and their children. Rose went to work at the paper mill as soon as she finished high school to support her family, and she never fulfilled any of her own personal dreams during her fifty-three years of work at the paper mill. When she went to work, her intelligence and motivation were so remarkable that she was promoted several times during her career, eventually leaving the mill floor for office work. Meanwhile, Rose never believed her success was the result of her abilities and competence. She asked me repeatedly, "What did they [the supervisors] see in me that I couldn't see in myself?" She reported that perhaps she would have gone to college if she had possessed what she calls "ambition." She says, "I don't know what I would have done if I'd had any ambition."

When I questioned her further about why she didn't go to college, her sister interrupted to say that the family "would have starved" without Rose's income. Rose objects, "I didn't know I had smart brains until a few people told me." Perhaps the answer lies in her early life because she has, as she says, "an inferiority complex." This may be attributed to her shame at being an illegitimate child. When I interviewed Rose, her sister was present for the first hour, and Rose was more reticent and cautious in her statements. As soon as her sister left, Rose informed me that she was born to an unwed mother. Throughout her life Rose has suffered from the stigma associated with her perceived status as an illegitimate child. She also considers herself to be a negative person.

> I guess I have always been a sort of a negative person. I didn't have nice clothes as the other kids did. We didn't have [the] money to. Sometimes we didn't have money to buy books because Mama, my mother, had to have all these medicines, and I always had a terrible inferiority complex. I was illegitimate, and I was four years old when my mother married again, well—married. And I was always aware of that [being illegitimate], and I always felt that everybody else was aware of it. That's one reason I felt so inferior. And that does something to a child.

Rose's perceived need to compensate for her illegitimate status and to help her family propelled her into a life of hard work, service, and self-sacrifice. Her mother was constantly ill, and so was unable to work, and Rose's stepfather did not maintain steady employment. "He tried, and he did the very best he could. [A lot of] my mother's illness was that she couldn't handle what had happened to her in the past. And that was not good for me, but I did what I could to help. And then when I started making money, I did help the girls get through school." Her family relied entirely on Rose for support. After her sisters were grown and independent, Rose provided money and personal care for her mother and stepfather until their deaths, and she continues to give money to her nieces and nephews, as well as to her sisters.

Rose also sacrificed herself for the company. During her fifty-three years at the paper mill, Rose was instrumental in maintaining continuity and competence through many administrations. "They thought I was crazy to work so much, but I just loved my work. For some people, work was just work, but I enjoyed mine. And I worked an awful lot of overtime. If I hadn't, they would've had to get somebody else." In addition, Rose took the initiative whenever she was faced with a problem or work need, stating, "I done a lot of things. In fact, I did a lot of things on my own." The people that she worked with recognized her capabilities, though, and promoted her through the years to an important administrative position in the company. However, she failed to see her own worth as a person and as an employee. "I could have done things a lot differently if I hadn't been so *downtrodden*, I mean, with my mind. [I would say] 'I'm not good enough for this.'" Though she did not respect her own work, she notes that "a *lot* of bosses would depend on me for a *lot* of things. I was always the person they came to before going to the superintendent of the company because I was there from the beginning of the company, and I had the continuity to do it right" (her emphasis). Rose had given all of her time, energy, and money to her family and to the company for fifty-three years in attempts to make up for her perceived inferiority. Now she lives alone in an old mobile home, not wanting or needing much in the way of comfort, still giving the majority of her money to others. After a career of sacrifice in the paper mill, Rose in her retirement continues to fill the role of family martyr.

SISTERS IN LABOR SACRIFICE

The narratives of self-sacrificing women in this project parallel the stories of their sisters in labor disputes, Ella May Wiggins and Crystal Lee Jordan, two well-known labor martyrs in North Carolina. Wiggins was killed for her attempts to unite the segregated black and white union locals in Gastonia and for her leadership in the Communist-affiliated National Textile Workers Union. Jordan, whose organizing efforts were popularized in the film *Norma Rae*, faced severe hardships, losing her reputation, her job, and her husband in the small town of Roanoke Rapids. These women have been the subject of documentaries and fictionalized accounts of their struggles. Their stories, intertwined with those of the women in this study, create a portrait of labor martyrs for an organized South.

Ella May Wiggins has been memorialized in many scholarly and fictional texts. Liston Pope, in his 1942 volume, *Millhands and Preachers*, includes a letter written by Wiggins. He uses her words to exemplify the "hidden resentment" that had been simmering in Gastonia and would erupt in open rebellion in 1929.

> I never made no more than nine dollars a week, and you can't do for a family on such money. I'm the mother of nine. Four died with the whooping cough. I was working nights, and I asked the super to put me on days, so's I could tend 'em when they had their bad spells. But he wouldn't. He's the sorriest man alive, I reckon. So I had to quit, and then there wasn't no money for medicine, and they just died. I couldn't do for my children any more than you women on the money we git. That's why I come out for the union, and why we all got to stand for the union, so's we can do better for our children, and they won't have lives like we got.[13]

Like Pope's earlier work, John Salmond's history of the Loray Mill Strike in *Gastonia 1929*, also tells the story of the labor heroine, including reactions to the death of Ella May Wiggins. "'The humble woman sought to improve the conditions under which she worked sixty hours a week to find bread for her five children,' and for this she had been slain."[14] Salmond states that Ella May Wiggins "was the true American."[15] He also notes that the union seemed to be the only path open to Wiggins as she struggled to improve her lot. "'In it she saw some hope for herself and her children, the possibility of a fuller life.'"[16] Like many of the journalists and historians he quotes, Salmond notes that Wiggins' death "made her a martyr, a symbol of the deeper meaning of the Gastonia struggle."[17]

Mary Heaton Vorse was one of the journalists who filed reports from Gastonia during the strike. She also wrote a fictionalized account of the dispute and Ella May Wiggins' story in her novel, *Strike!,* published in 1930. As historical fiction, this volume is one of a handful that tells a thinly-veiled story of labor heroine Wiggins and the Loray Mill Strike of 1929. A noted labor journalist and novelist prior to her assignment in Gaston County, Vorse wrote the novel with an apparent goal of reporting the news events through the lens of an outsider-turned-insider. Her tale features a male journalist, Roger Hewlett, as the protagonist, and readers experience the events and characters of this cataclysmic episode in labor history through his eyes. Throughout the novel, readers can imagine Vorse in this role, reporting stories about the lives of the long-suffering mountain folk who become millworkers and the heroics of the struggling young union organizers from the North. "With a spirit of adventure, Roger Hewlett got an assignment to do an article about the textile strike in Stonerton [Gastonia]. The strike had been going on for two weeks, and had been in the papers from the

sister] craved water. She could have been burning on the inside, you know, if she swallowed those flames. And Mama gave her a little bit of water. She took that swallow of water and laid down and it killed her." The horror of this event shadowed the family for many years afterwards; indeed, it has shaped much of Katherine's life. "Mama kept those clothes that she burn in for *years and years and years.* I was grown, and she still had those clothes, wrapped 'em up. What was it? A toboggan hat she wear and pinned up in there and her four pennies that somebody had give her in a little aspirin box, you know back then you got a little metal box. And Mama kept them for *years and years.*" Keepsakes of her sister's short and tragic life have also been stored in Katherine's heart ever since that time. In response, her adult life has been one of constant sacrifice for others, whether during illnesses or caring for their small children. She is always actively helping others, perhaps to atone for what she perceives to be her role in her sister's death.

Katherine's adult life has been consumed in service to others. In 1958 after the strike ended, Katherine married a man who had three children from a previous marriage. At that time Katherine had one daughter from an unexplained prior relationship, so I do not know whether she had been married to her daughter's father. After their marriage, her new husband moved Katherine and her daughter to his home in an isolated rural area, away from the close-knit community that she knew. While there, Katherine reports that her husband "did not stay home much." She was left alone with four small children to care for, lacking her customary support network. After living three or four years in this arrangement, Katherine left her husband and returned to the mill village. "I got disgusted down there so far, being in the country and all, I moved from down there and bought a house up in the city. And I moved up there." However, she and her husband never divorced, and when he became ill many years later, she took care of him. "He got sick and then he come—we never got divorced—he come to live with me, and I took care of him until he died. I was working at the hospital, and I stopped my work, took a leave, and took care of him. He was in a wheelchair, and he was on oxygen twenty-four hours [a day]." She later remarked that her father also had been wheelchair-bound, and she took care of him for a year until his death. Her last husband was also confined to a wheelchair and was completely paralyzed. Not only did she take care of these men in their illnesses and infirmities, Katherine also took care of children in her home at the same time. She stated that her estranged husband of twenty-five years finally had something good to say about her after she took him in. "And I come back and all the years I'd been married to him, he never said anything good about me. Always in his way, he was just always gone. That's one reason I left and moved to the city."

While she was caring for him during his illness, Katherine's husband remarked that he knew why the "good Lord" had kept him alive all those years. When Katherine asked him why, he replied, "'Because you always doing something good for somebody else.'" She says that she "about fell off the porch" when he said that because he had never before offered any words of gratitude or kindness. Katherine commented that the time while he was helpless was the best part of their marriage and that she enjoyed taking care of him as one would care for a child. "That was the best part of our marriage out of twenty-nine years when I had to shave him and bathe him and brush his teeth, comb his hair, feed him, do everything for him." When people asked her how she could have gone back to this long-estranged husband who had not been a loving partner in the early years before their separation, she said that her faith sustained her during this difficult time. "I had God inside of me, that made the difference, you know. And you know when God comes in, love comes in. You've got the love of God and you'll do a lot of things that you wouldn't have did if you weren't serving God."

Katherine has acted in accordance with her spiritual beliefs in her service to others. Whenever anyone needed her, Katherine would offer assistance, even if it meant getting little or no sleep for weeks and months.

> I used to leave home going to work at three in the afternoon. And I'd work from three o'clock until eleven o'clock at night. I would clock out at eleven and go do private duty with somebody, and work from eleven at night until seven the next morning. I would leave there and go to a house [where] the woman had had a stroke. And I just couldn't turn 'em down. They asked me to come and stay. I'd already had one back surgery. I've had two back surgeries, and I had one then. So I just couldn't say no.

In addition to sitting with sick people, Katherine would clean their homes and take care of personal hygiene for the patients. "I cleaned. I laid down on my stomach and took a vacuum and went under them beds. Nobody had cleaned in *years and years*, but they had money. Of course, I had to give [the patient] a bath every morning and I fixed his and her breakfast." Whenever other people asked if she would come help them, Katherine said that she couldn't refuse them. "I didn't want to go, but I couldn't say no. I stayed all night with them, and sometimes when you did double duty at the hospital, you were up and down all night long. You'd already worked eight hours, and you were about beat."

In between work and volunteering her time, Katherine also helped her neighbors with their lawn care and cleaning. Yet Katherine did not think that what she had done was remarkable. "I never thought I did anything.

I know sometimes people'd say, 'You did so much for me.' I said, 'I don't feel like I do anything.' You know, what I do, I'm glad to try to do what I can. But I don't feel like it's enough. But anyway I'm glad the Lord has given me the strength to be able to do the things that I do." Katherine has lived a life of unending service to others, including her two last husbands and her father, all of whom were paralyzed. With her last husband, she says that she did not sleep for three years while attending to his needs day and night and taking care of children during the day. "For three years I didn't go to bed." Whether for husbands, children, patients, or neighbors, Katherine has sacrificed her entire life to the needs of others.

Katherine and other workers often identify with their employers and the people in power. They have accepted the propaganda, and having no alternatives, choose to believe that their work lives are good. Even Katherine contends that the mill owners were gracious and generous people who enabled her parents to have a good life even though two of their children died, Katherine's younger sister, from the accident, and later, a younger brother, of pneumonia. She says, "Everbody helped everbody, 'cause we was all family, you know. And you worked with them, and you helped somebody, they helped you. We all worked together you know. And the Coopers were real nice people to their people that worked in the mill. They never bothered me out there." Although she emphasizes the beneficence of the mill owners, Katherine did not go back in the mill after the strike.

ELLA MAY WIGGINS: MARTYR FOR AN ORGANIZED SOUTH

In *Strike!*, originally published in 1930, Mary Heaton Vorse writes about similar difficulties, including workers whose children die of pellagra because of malnourishment. In reality, Ella May Wiggins had four of her nine children to die from whooping cough and other ailments, the result of poor nutrition and substandard housing, conditions which were exacerbated by Wiggins' long working hours when the children were unsupervised. Vorse describes the living conditions of Wiggins' fictional persona Mamie Lewes: "She lived in a blackened cabin way out of town. She and her children had one room and her cousin and his wife had taken the other room."[21] She tells Roger Hewlett that her children had never gone to school since she needed the only one old enough to attend school to take care of the younger children. Life is hard for Mamie and the thousands of mill women that she represents.

Vorse also devotes much of her novel to depictions of the strong and capable mill women who are striking alongside the men. She portrays them as the hope of the union in Stonerton, and even though they are frightened, these women fight with all of their intelligence, fortitude, and courage. Vorse says that they are essential to the union cause. Early in the novel, this focus is apparent. Irma says, "I think the women are pluckier than the men . . . They've got fighting stuff in them, these women."[22] In her novel, old women, young girls, women who are ill or overcome with grief, and women without hope all persevere in the strike, against the terrible odds that face them.

> In the picket line and parade, wherever workers meet together and have one another's support, it is easy enough to be militant, but when you are alone in the dark and your things are on the ground being rained on you'd expect people's spirit to be dampened. But these people's were not. All of them had courage. It was as if they said, "Nothing you can do to us is going to shake us." Doris, as if she read Roger's thoughts, turned to him and snapped at in a voice that was rendered hoarse with fatigue. "These women are militant workers."[23]

Throughout the novel, Vorse shows women as the backbone of the work being done to organize and strike for workers' rights.

Mamie Lewes is depicted as a woman who has overcome numerous hardships. She undergoes a marked transformation during the novel. At the beginning she is an innocent, shy woman who is unlikely to join the union. She is so poor that she cannot even afford to live in a mill house, and her children are endangered because she has to leave them alone while she works. Because she needs the oldest child to care for the younger ones, her daughter does not attend school. The downtrodden family remains under the dominion of poverty. However, Mamie's involvement with the union during the strike is portrayed as poignant, heart-felt, and pure. Mamie Lewes is a sacrificial victim, murdered by citizen vigilantes, the Committee of One Hundred, when she is traveling to a union meeting. "Here was the victim that the mob demanded. They had shot the singing woman to death. Blood was spreading over her bosom and over her dress."[24] This was also true of the real Ella May Wiggins, and her death, unlike Vorse's portrayal, was ordered specifically because of her work with organizing and uniting the black and white unions in Gaston County. Vorse's character Mamie does not live in a black section of town though Wiggins and her children did. She does however depict Mamie as an involved and dedicated union worker who contributes her natural singing and song-writing talents to the cause. "She and her 'song ballits' had been the very core of the strike . . . Now she was dead."[25] Mamie's death and funeral are similar to accounts of the real historical events on which they are based.

Strike!, a radical feminist novel, arrived on the literary and social scene in 1930 as a testament to the women and men who labored and lost in the violent strikes during 1929 in Gastonia and all across the South. Vorse, through Roger Hewlett's "objective" voice, offers her readers a sympathetic view of the workers' lives and situations, but her primary goal was to elicit a logical response to the unnecessary tragic defeat and deaths of workers struggling for the right merely to survive, to achieve a living wage. Through Roger Hewlett, Vorse enables her readers to think with him, to begin as observers and to end as activists. This development is subtle and powerful. Because it is an account, as a journalist would report, Vorse's readers can experience the immediacy of the events and more easily understand the forces that oppress the workers. What Vorse fails to show, however, is that the National Textile Workers Union was a Communist organization, a major reason for its being violently opposed by the business community. Though she was herself a member of the Communist Party, Vorse discreetly glosses over this fact in the novel. Only one incident reflects a Communist sensibility. This occurs when a union organizer's wife takes the witness stand to defend her husband in a murder trial. During questioning, the woman admits that she is an atheist, a fact that damns her testimony with both judge and jury. Vorse's oblique reference to the Communist Party obscures its importance in the events of 1929.

THE POWER OF THE MOB

Vorse described the political and social environment that led to the unrest and violence in Gastonia in 1929. She understood the mob mentality that accompanies large-scale violence. Her explanation of the mob behavior is an interesting aspect of the novel. Through her protagonist Roger, Vorse exposes the vicious reactions of the mob in Stonerton. Roger's tone conveys its larger import and the universal lesson. "Outside the mob waited. The mob was like an animal sitting on its haunches with its red tongue lolling out. The mob was a crazy man, yelling. This was his own secret hidden knowledge."[26] Later on, he notes that the Committee of One Hundred is an evil loosed in the world. "A long procession of hate. People out to destroy. A mob in cars sweeping through the country. Murder sweeping through the country, open and noisy, searching for its prey."[27] When Mamie Lewes is killed by the mob, her friend and fellow striker, having felt the hatred of the mob himself, considers how it could have happened. "What made mob? Who were mob? What had killed Mamie Lewes?"[28] When a woman asks him later who killed Mamie, he thinks, "It was as though a light had exploded within him. Every one was guilty. Every one who thought mob, or hate was guilty." He tells the woman, "'You all killed her! . . . 'This town killed her!'"[29] His words also convey Vorse's indictment of the violence.

SOUTHERN WORKER FOR SOCIAL JUSTICE

Like Mary Heaton Vorse, Myra Page was a writer and social activist who came to Gastonia in 1929 to cover the Loray Mill strike. Unlike Vorse, however, Page was a southerner whose work throughout her life had been to empower women and to promote the interests of the working-class, ultimately as an active member of the Communist Party. In 1932, Page's novel, *Gathering Storm*, a fictionalized version of Ella May Wiggins' story and the Gastonia conflict, was published. Prior to the strike, Page had been involved in the Young Women's Christian Association (YWCA) as a race relations and labor activist, ultimately uniting black and white women and educating them about economic systems and union participation. In her biography, Page recalled, "[M]any of us felt that the future of the country lay in the workers getting organized and making sensible reform in the country."[30]

As an industrial secretary for the YWCA, Page visited textile mills to learn more about women and work issues. Her first visit to a silk mill provided the insights that sparked her long career in labor activism. "When I saw the mill conditions and what the girls and women did day after day, I understood the need for unions."[31] During her experiences studying and working with Anarchists and intellectuals in New York, Page held a job in a men's clothing shop. She recalled their solidarity. "We were workers bound together in one great movement—comrades and equals . . . I discovered that working people wanted the right things for their children and the human race. I also discovered that unions could make life better, not only for those in them, but for those who weren't."[32] Page later earned a doctorate in sociology, completing a dissertation on textile workers in the Carolinas. Her research was published as *Southern Cotton Mills and Labor* in 1926. These experiences provided the background knowledge for her novel about the Gastonia strike.

Page wrote *Gathering Storm* from a sociologist's perspective, incorporating elements of race relations, child labor, and socialism. Her characters attempt to cross the color line and unite their efforts, only to be prevented by the political and economic structures of their community. Tom develops an awareness of the injustices of racism and realizes how he has been indoctrinated in the special brand of southern racism.

> Gradually Tom took to hanging out more at wobbly [*sic*] headquarters and reading the pamphlets and books which Jake left conveniently about. And there were many arguments. One constant topic was that of race.

Step by step Jake won ground and Tom was forced to give in, gradually at first but as the new world of ideas opened up, he found himself following Jake's lead with some eagerness. As Jake had told him, "Once a southern worker, white or black, gets it straight, he'll go the limit—once he sees how it's held us back."[33]

In addition to the race relations controversy, Page also examines the role of religion in the lives of working-class southerners. The mill-owned churches often hired ministers who urged their flocks not to strike or be involved in the union. "[The] local pastors went from house to house counseling the villagers. 'Remember the words of our Lawd Jesus. Let both sides forgive 'n forget.' 'My poor people, your feelin's mislead you. You've struck the hand that feeds you. Go back, while thar is still time.'"[34]

In Page's novel, Ella May Wiggins is depicted as a loving mother, balladeer, and labor activist. Wiggins inspires the crowd of unionists at a rally, singing her famous ballad, "Mill Mother's Lament." She also addresses the group, saying, "'We mill hands are a rovin' lot. At last we got our Union, somethin' to stick to, 'n that'll stick by us.'"[35] Highlighting the class struggle between mill workers and owners, *Gathering Storm* reaches a climax when labor heroine Wiggins dies in an ambush, killed by anti-union vigilantes. "Ella May clutched at her chest, 'They've shot me.' . . . Before they could get her to a hospital, Ella May was dead. 'They killed our singin' 'oman,' the mill hands said, 'we'll not forget. They killed her a-purpose.'"[36] The novel brings together the major sociological perspectives of the strike and southern textile workers: race, religion, and class. Myra Page, a Communist and labor activist, provides the means for her readers in the United States and abroad to consider the implications of racial inequality, corrupt religion, and unchecked capitalism.

THE SOCIOLOGY OF THE WORKING CLASS

Grace Lumpkin, herself a southerner and compatriot in the Communist Party, also penned a novel about the Gastonia conflict. Lumpkin's *To Make My Bread*, as did *Gathering Storm*, provides a sociological approach to the problem of workers' rights. The novel, also published in 1932, offers insights into the lives of the mountain people who moved into the mill towns. Fully half of her novel is set in the mountains, a prologue for the cataclysmic events to come. Her Appalachian characters are portrayed as fiercely independent people who, despite their harsh existence, are proud and loyal to family and friends. Lumpkin's sympathetic portrait includes their dire economic situation and the subsequent loss of their land to outsiders who cheated them. This exploitation foreshadows the obstacles they will face as textile wage slaves. After their move to the mill towns, the mountain people continue to live in poverty, more difficult to bear because they have also lost their prized independence. Lumpkin depicts the mountain people's lives in an ethnographic style. The reader, like Lumpkin's narrator, shares the experiences of the remote, impoverished, and independent world of the mountain folk. The character Grandpap teaches the children that they are free people if they own land. "'You're free men . . . so long as you've got your own potato patch and house and a gun.'"[37]

In the novel Lumpkin shows not only the negative, hard-scrabbling life of these people; she also portrays them as fun-loving and appreciative of the natural beauty that surrounds them. Grandpap's most prized possession is his fiddle, and folks gather at the family cabin to dance and sing together whenever they can. They also work together, and their solidarity is evident, sustaining them in the mill villages where they encounter new hardships. Ultimately, this family—emblematic of thousands of other families—struggles together, both in their mountain homeland and in the mill town. Unlike Vorse's attempt to achieve a factual, objective account of the Gastonia strike, Lumpkin makes the conflict more personal, showing the sensory effects of their lives, as when the family is starving during a snowstorm.

> For the first time John knew what it meant to have pains in his belly because it was empty. He had been hungry before for a day perhaps, but Grandpap had always managed to provide something. Now his belly had been empty for three days. The pains were grasshoppers jumping from one blade of grass to another. They hopped from one place to another in his belly and each time they lit a sharp pain struck him. Bonnie felt the pains. She sat in a corner with her arms pressed tightly over her belly. She was trying to hold the grasshoppers from jumping. Emma watched them. There was nothing for her to do but watch.[38]

Lumpkin's accounts of the workers' hardships are distressing to the reader because of the immediacy afforded through sensory descriptions and a first-person perspective.

INDEPENDENCE AND CHANGE

The McClure family moves to the mill town because of the promise of riches, an easier life, and freedom from the vagaries of subsistence farming. Each member of the family finds a way to cope with the harsh circumstances of life on the farm and in the town. For Basil, escape comes through religion and education. He aligns himself with a fundamentalist preacher who rebukes Grandpap for his "sinful" ways. Basil is no longer loyal to his family. He grows to feel disdain for them, and he leaves home to become a preacher himself. For Grandpap, the coping strategy is whiskey. When the family needs money, he resorts to making "corn mash" to sell for "bootleg" whiskey, and he also drinks it when he wishes to escape his plight. However, his escape is short-lived because he is sentenced to one year in prison when he is caught. To escape his own woes, Kirk follows in Grandpap's path: drinking and selling whiskey. Kirk also rescues a "bad" woman who is pregnant with another man's child. The woman continues the relationship with her lover after her marriage to Kirk. When he finds his wife and her lover together, the man shoots and kills Kirk. The McClure family, reeling from the loss of all of its men, is in a dire situation. John, though not yet old enough to do so, assumes the male responsibilities of the farm, and Basil becomes the legal heir. Basil claims the property and sells it to a logging company. His decision forces the family to move to the mill town to find work. In the town, the McClures no longer have any control over their lives and the conditions of their labor. Though poor in their mountain home, at least they had autonomy and independence. In the mill village, they become entrapped in an oppressive economic and social system, one that continued to exploit workers in the following decades.

CRYSTAL LEE JORDAN: THE SACRIFICES OF "MILL TRASH"

Just as the fictionalized accounts of Ella May Wiggins in the 1920s reveal real hardships, sacrifices, and losses for working-class people, the true accounts of Crystal Lee Jordan's life demonstrate that the struggle for justice in textile mills continued into the late twentieth century. As Henry Liefermann explains in his biography, *Crystal Lee: A Woman of Inheritance,* Jordan was born into a family employed in textile mills in Roanoke Rapids, North Carolina. Growing up in this small mill town, Jordan's family suffered financial hardships and the degradation of being considered mill "trash." As was true for most mill workers, they lived in a small, company-owned house.

> The Pulleys' first home in Roanoke Rapids was a graying wood-frame duplex at 316 B Monroe Street, a short walk from Albert Pulley's job at Roanoke Mill #2. Odell Pulley's parents lived with them, and the four children and four adults filled every corner in their half of the small house. The mill owned the house. The mill owned every

other house in town, each house the same distance from its neighbors . . . [39]

The family had limited income as well as personal strife. Jordan's father
was a hard-drinking, angry man. Both of her parents worked in the mill,
her mother on the third shift, and her father on first. When Jordan was in
the eleventh grade, she also began working full-time in the mill on the second shift. "When Crystal Lee got home from school in the afternoon, she
had just enough time to change to work clothes and leave."[40] Her work
in the mill continued after high school graduation and her early marriage
at age nineteen to Junior Wood. In those early years, Jordan struggled
with several hardships, including strenuous work, physical abuse from
her husband, the stress of a new baby, and a bitter marital separation.
Working to overcome these difficulties, she and Junior had worked to
rebuild their relationship slowly and were attempting to reconcile when
Junior died as a rresult of an automobile accident. Jordan's grief caused
her to seek comfort in a love affair with a wealthy former classmate. He
was a student at UNC Chapel Hill and was home to visit. She became
pregnant with his child, but Jordan would not marry him even though he
asked her. This decision was just one of many that would affect her life in
dramatic ways.

Even before she joined efforts to unionize the J.P. Stevens plant in
Roanoke Rapids, Jordan endured many sacrifices, including losing her
reputation, her education, and her marriage. When her second child was
born out of wedlock, Jordan faced the moral judgments of life in a small
town. Eventually she married Cookie Jordan, and they had a child. Bored
and needing money for her family, Jordan tried working in the service
industry, both as a hostess in a "gentleman's club" and as a waitress.
She "began catering at country club parties," still feeling uncomfortable.[41] "The feelings from her childhood—that she was not as good as the
people who joined country clubs—bothered her."[42] When a mill supervisor began flirting with Jordan, she knew that she must quit that job
and return to mill work. "It was not that work in the cotton mills was
easier than the restaurant, nor that it paid more. It was harder work, she
knew from experience, and the wages, while predictable, were not better
than her worst weeks in the restaurant and not nearly as good as those
weeks when tips were high."[43] However, Jordan was "comfortable in the
mills."[44] She went back to work folding towels five and six nights a week
for eight hours each night. "Most of her friends, and almost every one of
her neighbors, worked there. She was born to working in the mills, she
thought. Her father had worked in the mills, and her mother still did.

Her brothers and sisters did. [Her husband] Cookie's entire family did."[45] Working in a cotton mill seemed the inevitable fate for Crystal Lee Jordan.

The Organizing Campaign

In 1973, Jordan was working at J.P. Stevens when the Textile Workers Union of America (TWUA) launched a campaign to organize at least half of the seventy-five Stevens mills in North Carolina. The company had been effective in illegally opposing union organizing efforts a decade earlier in 1963, resulting in "dozens of charges against JP [Stevens] by the union in federal courts in the South."[46] One of the charges—that workers were illegally fired for joining the union—led to a judgment requiring Stevens to pay tens of thousands of dollars in back pay to those workers. In addition, Stevens was forced to issue an embarrassing apology to all of those workers. The apology letter "also had to be posted on every bulletin board in every Stevens mill."[47] The court determined the exact wording of the apology.

> There never had been anything like it in the history of the cotton mills, nor the history of organized labor. But whether the court order would lead to union victories was another question. Textiles was the only basic industry in the nation that was not unionized; only 10 percent of the 700,000 Southern mill hands belonged to the TWUA. The union's campaign against Stevens, begun in 1963, had by 1973 won an election at only one plant. It was not that the mill hands did not want to join the union, but that Stevens intimidated them from doing so. That was the reason the union gave, and in part at least the union was right.[48]

Because of the letter and her own ideas about working in a cotton mill, Jordan began to consider what union membership could mean for her and her fellow workers.

Taking a friend with her, Jordan attended a union organizing meeting at a black church in a remote rural location. She and her friend were the only two white people at the meeting. Eli Zivkovich, the union representative who had spent twenty years helping organize coal miners, noticed Jordan's enthusiastic interest in the union. He invited Jordan to become a local organizer. She began to talk to other workers during breaks and at lunch. "I started in the canteens, on break time . . . I would talk union to my friends, and I started getting a lot of membership cards signed."[49] Jordan also helped Zivkovich and the other TWUA officers know how the company was reacting to the union drive. In response to the union activity, the plant manager posted a threatening four-page letter on a company bulletin board. The letter was especially intimidating to African American workers because in addition to the "usual anti-union messages," the letter depicted black unionists as an angry, militant group. Since 80 percent of the workers were white, the management hoped to discredit the union by pandering to the racism among the white workers. If the white workers thought that the union was a "black" enterprise, the organizing drive would be defeated. Because the union needed a copy of the letter, Zivkovich asked Jordan to copy it, a difficult task since the bulletin board was near supervisors' offices. Copying the letter was considered hostile to the company, and Jordan could only record parts of it at a time during breaks and lunch. When she was observed copying the letter, her supervisor told her to stop. Later the plant manager called Jordan to his office and ordered her not to copy the letter, but she completed her task, boldly defiant in the face of intimidation by management.

"The Mother Jones of the Textile Union"

Jordan was later ordered to leave the plant, but she refused. When the manager threatened to call the police and have her forcibly removed from the property, Jordan said that he should call her cousin's husband who was the chief of police because her husband Cookie was a very jealous man. She walked out into the plant and successfully resisted a security guard's attempt to prevent her from returning to work. She arrived at her table with most of the other workers watching her. They had heard about Jordan's confrontation with supervisors, so they knew what was going on. When a city police officer arrived, Jordan resisted him as well.

> Crystal Lee kept looking at him as she pulled from the tabletop a sheet of stiff cardboard, one of the inserts used in packing. She picked up a black marking pencil from the table and began writing on the cardboard, in heavy, block letters. The cop came no closer. Crystal Lee hoisted herself onto the tabletop, then stood up on it. She held her sign high over her head, in both hands, and slowly turned in a circle so the mill hands on the open floor, the women in put-up, the side hemmers and terry cutters, all of them watching her now, could read what she had written: "UNION."[50]

Jordan was subsequently fired and began working full-time for the union organizing campaign. Just as Ella May Wiggins had done in the Gastonia conflict decades earlier, Jordan brought black and white workers together in the campaign. Zivkovich described her as the "Mother Jones of the textile union."[51] In 1974, the union was approved by a narrow margin of votes, but the victory was attributed to the efforts, and ultimately the sacrifices, of Crystal Lee Jordan.

ANNIE: SACRIFICING KITH AND KIN

Like Ella May Wiggins and Crystal Lee Jordan, Annie faced the wrath of people in her small town because of her union organizing attempts. Annie is a twice-retired textile employee who participated in the General Textile Strike of 1934 as a "scab," or replacement worker. Her work within the context of that historical event takes an interesting turn later in her narrative. In 1934, Annie was a fifteen-year-old child whose father had abandoned the family, the first major disruption in her life. Annie was the oldest of three children whose mother was unable to work because of illness. Since she was under the legal age, Annie was unable to collect her pay, so the mill management "hired" her, withholding her pay for two months until she turned sixteen. After the strike was over, she was a trained worker, with a paying job and a willingness to do, as she says, "whatever it takes" to get the work done. Another major historical event, World War II, led Annie in a different direction. She was recruited, along with other women working in the textile mill, to work in Charlotte at a munitions factory. A true-life "Rosie the Riveter," Annie then worked at a union plant and eventually became shop steward. The women in her area called for a "wildcat," or unsanctioned, strike because they found out that the men were making more money per hour than they were. Annie told the women that she would talk to union officials about the situation before they went out on strike. When the union was able to negotiate wage equity for the women in the company, Annie realized the benefits of membership in a union.

After the war, she returned to her textile mill job, eager to learn more about unions. When enough workers at her factory had joined the union in 1950, the union leaders called for an election. During the time of the union organizing effort, Annie was targeted by management for her involvement since she had invited organizers to stay in her home where she also hosted union meetings. When she later missed a day of work because her child was sick, Annie was illegally fired. She took her case to the National Labor Relations Board who defended her and for five other workers who were terminated illegally for union activity. Not to be deterred, Annie fought the company for six years, finally winning her case. The company paid her all six years' back wages and reinstated her with seniority at her old job in the "warper room." It should be noted that while she was unemployed during that six-year period, Annie could not find work elsewhere. She was, as she recalls, "blackballed," or blacklisted, which meant that the mill superintendent had called other companies in the area and told them not to hire Annie because she was a "troublemaker." Her inability to work hurt her as much as any of the other difficulties that she had faced. Since much of Annie's identity is constructed by her working life, the loss of her ability to work was an especially cruel blow. She said, "All I wanted to do was work. But I didn't back off. I never would say that I would do what they wanted me to do [to be reinstated]." Thus Annie has experienced both personal exigencies that caused her to cross the picket line in one dispute, and she has witnessed the power of solidarity to change conditions for the better in another. Throughout her ordeals, Annie suffered personal losses of several kinds, becoming a martyr for organized labor in her small town.

The silences inherent in Annie's narrative are indicative of the times when she was in dismal straits in her early family life and later when she was ostracized for her political views. In both the General Textile Strike of 1934 as a "scab" and in 1950 as a union organizer, Annie was vilified by the people in her community. This may account for her silences during her young adulthood and the twenty missing years after she was legally laid off from her job at the mill when she was forty-one years old. Her narrative resumes at age sixty-two when she retired from another manufacturing plant in the area. After her first retirement, she spent the next nine years working full-time for the town government, managing the clubhouse at a public golf course. She retired a second time at age seventy-one. Throughout her years of working and taking care of her children, Annie sacrificed for what she believed was right, even when it meant that she would become an outcast in her hometown. Currently she works part-time at a retirement home and volunteers to lead senior activities, including bingo. Meanwhile, she sews and quilts for grandchildren, friends, and neighbors.

Family Betrayal

While the community's ostracism caused Annie great pain, the primary story of loss that undergirds her narrative involves betrayal by her brother, a supervisor at the mill. When Annie filed her case with the National Labor Relations Board, the company sent her brother to negotiate with her. Her narrative is filled with references to "Archer Manning," (a pseudonym) her brother, though early in her story she doesn't claim him as a sibling. Advocating for herself meant that Annie had to stand alone against her brother, one of three family members that she had supported as the sole wage earner beginning when she was fifteen years old. She sacrificed her education and her youth to help take care of him, only to be repaid years later with his betrayal. When the company communicated with her, it did so through her brother, who would go to Annie's house early in the morning after her husband left for work. "I knew [Archer Manning] had something to do with [the mill's case]." This is the first introduction of him in Annie's narrative, spoken as though he were unrelated to her. Throughout her story, Annie repeatedly describes interactions and bargaining with him:

> [Archer Manning], my brother, came to my home and said, "I hate to see you get messed up in this union business. Why don't you get out and get on the winning side? If the election had been held a month ago [before they fired six people for organizing], they might have won, but not now. I think I have enough influence with [the head of the mill] to get you back to work if you will go back and withdraw from the union and drop your charges against the company."

Annie tells him that she knows that he is just "doing what they're telling you to keep your job." Annie bargains with her brother for a meeting with the "higher ups," but this is really her strategy to learn what they are willing to offer. She had no intentions of dropping either her membership in the union or her charges against the company. Her unwavering strength, fierce survival instincts, and belief in justice led to this second rupture in her family life—with her brother. This struggle cost her much, and she sacrificed family relationships to pursue a just cause while defending herself against the oppressive mill owners.

Loss of Work Identity

The selectivities in Annie's narrative include emphasizing her work, especially pride in her work when the mill supervisors attempted to disparage her during the lawsuit. She spoke of her work: "The job was one warper, and what they called a twist warper, and baby, I would have on a whole warp which was maybe five, ten thousand yards, and the [other] guy wouldn't have but one thread. If one thread broke, it would stop it off." She also spoke at length about being ostracized by other workers and about the disruption with her brother. When she returned to work after the National Labor Relations Board lawsuit was settled, Annie said that she knew that she would not be welcome.

> The lawyer asked me, "[Annie], would you really go back to work?" I said that would be happiest day of my life, the day I walk back to that mill. I said I give 'em all these years, and I said, "Yes, the day I walk

back in that mill will be the happiest day of my life." I walked in there
that night at eleven o'clock, and I'd always go in, and we'd set down
on beams, maybe two or three of them together. And I knew I'd be
snubbed up that night. That didn't bother me one bit. Oh yes, I knew
I'd be snubbed that night specially.

Though Annie adamantly states that she was unaffected by these conflicts,
even within her family, her narrative is filled with these references, indicating that much of her life has been shaped by these sacrifices. "I knowed him
all my life, but honey, it didn't bother me none if the rest of them talked to
me or not." She adds, "I done showed 'em that I wasn't going to set back
and take what they wanted to give me after all these years."

She spoke little about her three daughters, both husbands, and her
family of origin, merely mentioning these facts. It is obvious that Annie has
been in a fight for survival, earning the right to walk proudly in her community. During our meeting, she read excerpts of the trial proceedings to
me, continuing to emphasize her innocence while criticizing the mill owners
and managers who threatened her at every turn during the six years of the
suit. The language of trials and retaliation, lying and proving oneself, and
fear and independence dominate Annie's narrative. These dialectical ideas
are threaded throughout her story. For example, winning the lawsuit is the
first thing Annie talked about during the interview. This triumph after years
of struggle for her right to work—a major factor in constructing her identity—is perhaps the defining moment of her life. In an attempt to defame
her, the mill management tried to portray Annie as an ineffective worker.
In telling this detail, Annie spluttered, "Now, honey, that was the biggest
lie. I put out more production than the rest of them the rest of the time."
She later repeated, "That was the biggest lie." When her former supervisor
told the review board that Annie "got in her eight hours," implying that
she got eight hours pay but that she did not work hard, Annie countered
with a strong assertion of her work record: "I could prove that I put out
more production on my warpers than any of the rest of them." During the
dispute, Annie eventually lost her reputation because she fought injustice,
sacrificing her livelihood and her standing in the community along with her
access to other jobs.

Annie spoke of the fear that influences other workers' behavior and
prevents them from joining the union. "People were scared to [join], and
they didn't know that much about the union. I'd say they were brain-
washed." On the other hand, Annie's courage and independence are also
woven into the fabric of her story. "I said you know when I go up there
[at the trial and ask], What it's going to be? I don't pull any punches." She

repeatedly showed her strength: "But I didn't back off; I didn't back off. I never would say that I would do what they wanted me to do." Later in her narrative, Annie recalled telling someone that "my girls don't make my decisions," and "I answer to nobody." Her sacrifices are tempered by her enduring spirit and long-lasting commitment to her work and her children. While Annie has suffered much, her martyrdom includes a community where workers never succeeded in organizing a union. Because of this, the workers—and the town—have lost even more.

THE SACRIFICES OF WORKING-CLASS WOMEN

In both the private and the public domains, working-class women often succumb to self-sacrifice, denying their own needs, dreams, and self-development to take care of others. While Noddings and Gilligan offer positive examples of women in their roles as care-givers and nurturers, they fail to account for the systematic patriarchal forces that affect the lives of working-class women. If a woman subsumes her own life for family members, friends, and neighbors, those endeavors do not necessarily reflect patriarchal oppression. However, in the world of work, patriarchy combined with capitalism leads to an unfair system that often further subjugates women. Labor organizers Ella May Wiggins and Crystal Lee Jordan, in their separate battles, endeavored to claim their power and to give agency to other workers. As Annie discovered in her work during World War II at a union plant, organized labor offers women the opportunity to address the inequities of the workplace, empowering women to assume their places at the bargaining table in a democratic environment. On the other hand, Rose and Katherine sacrificed their entire lives for their companies, their patients, and for their family members, choosing to accept the conditions imposed on their labors and their lives. In contrast, Annie sacrificed her family relationships, her reputation in town, and her identity as a worker through a long battle with a large textile company. Because she successfully resisted these forces, her martyrdom is not self-imposed; rather Annie's fight for justice leads to betrayal while she retains her dignity and self-worth. Regardless of the circumstances and the choices made by each of them, the lives of women in these labor struggles are characterized by sacrifice and loss.

Chapter Six

"I Do the Politics":
Union Feminism and Social Justice

Women's participation in unions in the United States during the past two centuries reflects the changes and challenges of organized labor and the women's movement during turbulent times in the nation's history. In the latter twentieth century, the two converge as union feminism, a viable strategy for women workers. Union feminism empowers them to challenge the inequities that continue to plague women in the workforce. Union feminists are weaving a strong and beautiful fabric to clothe themselves as collectively they pursue gender equality and workplace democracy for all working-class people. The women in this study work or have worked in various settings, in divergent industries, and in different periods of history, and they espouse equally diverse views on feminism. Indeed in some cases, they may not even claim an awareness of feminist concerns. However, the effects of the feminist movement in each of their lives is evident, as with the first wave of feminism, which provided for their enfranchisement, at least in the case of white women. For women of color and immigrants, however, both the South and the North effectively silenced their political voices through state laws and intimidation. Two of the women who participated in this project were born prior to the passage of the 19th Amendment, so their sensibilities likely are different from those of the younger women. As a result of the second wave of feminism, which divided women along class lines rather than by color and national origin, the women in this study gained greater access to trades dominated by men although these better-paying jobs continue largely to be held by their male counterparts.

The third wave of feminism, represented here in the form of union feminism, situates the women in this study on common ground. According to Diane Balser in *Sisterhood and Solidarity: Feminism and Labor in Modern Times*, "[b]ringing together the feminist and union movements could be a major key to broad societal change" since "women make up the majority of the working class, and are close to becoming 50 percent of the wage-workers."[1] This coalition unites disparate groups in their common goals of equity and empowerment in the workplace. As Maxine Greene suggests in *The Dialectic of Freedom*, "When we think of the diverse and pluralist society . . . , we need then to have in mind a range of individuals or groups confronting a field of possibilities in which varied ways of behaving and reacting may be realized. Against such a background, power and action cannot but resist doctrines of determinism . . . "[2]

Fueled by the power of self-determining women workers who are united by feminism, a more democratic workplace may be achieved, and a more inclusive, equitable society may be formed. Union feminism represents the multiple viewpoints and includes the divergent voices of feminism, ultimately affording working-class women the means to achieve agency in their work and in their personal lives. As with their sister organizers in the past, three of the women in this study—Millie, Kim, and Ellen—emerge as deft weavers of union feminism, assisting their union sisters in crafting a new fabric of hope and resistance in the labor and feminist movements.

Though both endeavored to overcome oppressive systems, the feminist and labor movements have not always worked together for the common good. The quest for political power is a function of both movements, but labor organizations have not always been advocates for women's rights. Under a patriarchal system, working women were in no better position within the male-dominated labor movement than they were in the non-union workplace. Diane Balser explains the connection between women's lack of power and patriarchal institutions. "Throughout the history of feminism there has been an understanding that gaining political power—in order to change society and control one's life is essential to free women from oppression. Feminist leaders have generally believed, from the earliest stages of the movement, that institutionalized powerlessness underlies female servitude."[3] Because of the rampant inequalities of women in the work world, unions now have a mandate to promote women's rights or risk alienating a large segment of their participant base. Balser notes, "Economic issues such as pay equity, the unionization of women workers, and increased social benefits have also become part of the larger women's liberation movement."[4] As the two movements come together to further the interests of working-class women, they have the power to forge a coalition with greater possibilities for improving the political power of all women. According to Balser, "Real economic power for women means organizing women in such a way that they can gain control over their economic lives, end inequality, and share fully in the society's material wealth and decision-making."[5] Far from having economic and political power, women long have been consigned to subservient roles.

Arising from the anti-slavery movement of the 1800s, the women's rights movement focused primarily on middle and upper class women's access to higher education and professional work. In *Feminist Theory: From Margin to Center*, bell hooks describes the exclusive focus of earlier activists.

> If improving conditions in the workplace for women had been a central agenda for the feminist movement in conjunction with efforts to obtain better-paying jobs for women and finding jobs for unemployed women of all classes, feminism would have been seen as a movement addressing the concerns of all women. Feminist focus on careerism, getting women employed in high-paying professions . . . alienated masses of women from feminist movement [*sic*]. . . . Had they looked at the economic situation of poor and working-class women, they would have seen the growing problem of unemployment and increased entry of women from all classes into the ranks of the poor.[6]

Caroline Dall, an activist in the early feminist movement, was also concerned with the rights of poor women and children. She published a book entitled, *Women's Rights to Labor* in 1859, insisting that women be given the right to work. "I ask for woman, then, free and untrammeled access to all fields of labor; and I ask it first on the ground that she needs to be fed . . . "[7] Dall further noted that women "want work for all the reasons that men want it."[8]

By the early 1900s women involved in the labor movement continued to emphasize their right to work. A paternalistic attitude prevailed, keeping women from being independent. Wages for women were extremely low. According to Nan Enstad in *Ladies of Labor, Girls of Adventure*, "Some employers went so far as to refuse to employ women who did not live with parents, because their wages could not support someone even at barest subsistence."[9] In addition the unions "dismissed women's actual struggles on the basis that their 'ideal' role was in the home. They often countered women's pleas for attention by telling them to go back home, an impossibility for most."[10] This paternalism created an activist sensibility among women. Increasingly they began to demand their rights, forming labor unions that were comprised largely of women workers, including the International Ladies' Garment Workers Union and the Women's Trade Union League, among others. Their political activity led to changes for all workers.

If public opinion deemed the striking women to be legitimate political actors with grievances, owners would be greatly pressured to bow
to union demands or risk losing sales. Therefore, strike leaders needed
to *politicize* striking women's grievances. . . . Strikers and leaders sought to make women's workplace grievances an issue of general
concern. . . . Ironically, working women's historical exclusion from the
arena of formal political exchange amplified leaders' willingness to speak
for them. . . . Thus, the experiences and understandings of striking
women themselves were not directly expressed. . . . [11]

It was not until the middle of the twentieth century that women workers were
ceded more rights and responsibilities within labor unions, in part the result of
the civil rights movement, the peace movement, and the women's movement.

Union feminism in its early stages shared much with other struggles of
the time. Writing about the peace movement of the 1960s, Shelley Douglass
notes: "'We were welcomed into the movement in lower-echelon positions, as
somebody's woman, girl, old lady, wife, as sex objects, as workhorses. Women
were expected to make coffee and provide refreshments while men planned
strategy and did resistance actions.'"[12] Just as their sisters had done in the
early labor movement of the 1930s, the women involved in the civil rights and
peace movements were still subject to oppressive sexism. Douglass explains:

"Women kept the homefires burning while men organized, acted, and
went to jail. Women bore and raised children and created the homes to
which the men returned. Women did leaflets in the thousands, typed letters, licked stamps, marched in demonstrations. We rarely spoke at demonstrations; our actions did not make us celebrities like the men. When
women went to jail, they lacked strong community support. They had no
knowledge, by and large, of their historic role in the peace movement."[13]

According to Lisa Leghorn in "The Economic Roots of the Violent Male
Culture," in Iceland in 1974, women "stopped doing paid and unpaid
work," with "90% of them gathering in public meetings to draw up lists of
demands."[14] While there was some opposition to women's consignment to
lesser roles, as in the Icelandic women's strike, the majority of women did
not collectively resist oppressive conditions. Women's feminist activism and
their work to make unions more inclusive and responsive to their interests and
needs have resulted in women's empowerment and leadership within union
power structures and politics.

The Canadian branch of the United Steel Workers of America (USWA)
is one notable example of the support that unions are beginning to afford

their women members. According to Ellen Bravo in "Going Public," the union begins every conference and convention, no matter the topic, with a presentation "defining what sexual harassment is and stating that it will not be tolerated at that meeting. Anyone violating this rule, it is announced, will be sent home with a letter to the local Executive Board detailing the offense."[15] This insistence on women's rights in the workplace is evident in the narratives of the USWA members in this study. Though in a small minority, both women hold leadership positions in their union local, whose female membership comprises ten percent of the nearly 1100 members. Positive changes for women workers are being implemented slowly to the ranks of labor unions in the United States.

Although overall union membership in the United States is declining, women's membership in unions is increasing. In "What Do Unions Do for Women?," Jill Braunstein and her colleagues report that trends are changing. Women comprise more than a third of union membership, currently 37 percent, for an all-time high for women unionists.[16] Men who are union members are more likely to be in "blue-collar" jobs while women are more likely to be in service industries. "Professional and technical workers are the largest single group of women union members."[17] The roots of women's participation in unions occurred during the Depression when discrimination increased dramatically against working women, especially those who were married. Nelson Lichtenstein and his fellow authors of the American Social History Project explain the problem.

> Many agreed with the man who signed himself, "A Good Citizen" in a letter to the president: "I know that something can be done about the married women. . . . They have no right taking the jobs and positions of single girls, single men, and married men." People assumed that married women worked only to make "pin money." That was rarely the case, but when layoffs occurred, even progressives thought that married women should be the first to go. Thus, both New England Telephone and Telegraph and the Northern Pacific Railroad fired all married women in 1931. In most cases married women were banned from teaching.[18]

Although the American Federation of Labor to some degree supported the discrimination against married women at least in part, the decade of the 1930s ushered in a new recruitment frenzy. According to Lichtenstein and his colleagues, unions recruited nearly a million women, "especially in the garment trades, electrical products, clerical and sales work, canning, and tobacco processing" during the Depression.[19] Women became leaders in labor disputes, organizing and participating in sit-down strikes in "hotels, drugstores, restaurants, and auto-parts factories."[20]

Women also played a significant role in connecting the union cause to people in the community through their participation on picket lines with husbands, fathers, and sons; through their work in soup kitchens and tenant organizations; and through education and entertainment programs. Their contributions led to a "dense, supportive social network that strengthened the ties of solidarity inside the factory and out."[21] Though women working in unions in the 1930s provided solidarity through social activism, their endeavors did not bring them equality. Feminist ideas were rejected in the union halls and in union politics. "Even in industries in which most workers were women, male union activists did not welcome female leadership."[22] In addition, at that time, pay inequities and lack of access to jobs continued to plague women in unions. Therefore, the women resorted to creating departments within their unions that focused on their distinct interests and needs, and they necessarily dropped the auxiliary work that had supported union causes, instead centering their activism in feminist issues.

UNION FEMINISM AND SOCIAL CHANGE

Labor researcher Diane Balser notes that the merging causes of feminism and unionism could lead to "broad societal change."[23] Since women comprise the majority of the working class, "we need to make ourselves aware of the potential power that would come from organizing women as workers."[24] The benefits of unionization are clear: according to Jill Braunstein and her colleagues, women in unions "earn an average of $2.50 an hour more than non-unionized women."[25] In addition, "women of color who are unionized earn 87 cents or 13 percent more than non-unionized women."[26] The pay inequities and lower job tenure evident in most fields are less likely for union women.

> There is a smaller pay gap between male and female workers in a unionized workforce ($2.77 per hour) than in a non-unionized workforce ($3.45 per hour). Unionized women earned 75 cents for every dollar earned by unionized men, while non-unionized women earned 68 cents for every dollar earned by non-unionized men. Unionization is also associated with greater job tenure. Unionized women workers have twice as many years on the job as non-union workers.[27]

Thus unions have provided their women workers with the greatest access to equality and social change in the workplace. Unions also educate their women members in leadership schools, offering workshops that reflect the continuum of knowledge and activism of most women. In "Teaching Leadership to Union Women: The Use of Stories," Michelle Kaminski notes that women leaders develop in four distinct stages. The first stage is "finding your voice" where a woman has sufficient self-esteem to speak up.[28] In the second stage, women learn basic skills such as writing and speaking in public and gaining technical knowledge, and in the third stage, women "learn how to get things done in the existing political context."[29] They apply this newfound political knowledge in their unions, workplaces, and communities. The fourth and final stage, mobilizing others, occurs when a woman leader begins developing and directing projects that others join. Her focus in the final stage is on "having a long-term impact."[30] The union feminists in this study have arrived at the fourth level whereby they empower other workers to achieve agency and to find their voices.

NORTH CAROLINA WOMEN AT WORK

Gender inequality—the impetus for feminisms of all kinds—emerges in the narratives of working-class women throughout American society. The women in this study reflect these inequities in the workplace. In many cases, the women experience direct and overt sexism and discrimination. For others, the inequalities are more subtly expressed, or they are nearly absent from the narratives entirely. In several instances, men acting as agents of feminism improve the working lives and the lived experiences of their female counterparts. Whether they would claim the tie to women's empowerment is another matter. However, in the narratives of the women involved in strikes in North Carolina, this is a rare occurrence. More often, women are subjected to degrading and dangerous ostracism. In her 2003 study of women in the steel industry, *Union Women: Forging Feminisms in the United Steelworkers of America,* Mary Margaret Fonow explores the sexism and discrimination that these women face. "How hostile was the work climate in the early years? Some women reported a no-win situation. 'If the guys talk to me, I talk to them. But I never go out of my way to talk to the men. If you don't talk to the guys, you are stuck up, conceited, a bitch. If you do talk to them, they say you are a whore. So you can't win.'"[31] Several of the women in this study faced this overt hostility and sexism and reported the pain and loneliness of their second-class status at work, especially in the male-dominated workplaces of tire manufacturing and telecommunications. Millie, Kim, and Ellen all have encountered discrimination in their work; however, each employs the power of union feminism to fight oppressive conditions and prove her worth on the job.

In addition, each has developed her own power while engaging her union sisters and brothers in acts of self-determination and solidarity.

MILLIE: PROVING HERSELF WORTHY

In addition to the sexual harassment and discrimination that women face in the largely male domains, many of the women must also prove their ability and their worth to "compete" with the men in "*their* work." Millie is a member of the United Steel Workers of America who works in a tire manufacturing plant in a large city in North Carolina. For Millie, the first day of work at the plant was challenging. She says, "I was a tire builder, and I had to build these [huge] tires. . . . [I've] gained weight now, but I was like that, just so skinny. Those guys *bet* that I wouldn't make it. Those men didn't know they gave me the incentive to stay. They said I wasn't going to make it, [but] I was one of the best tire builders they had." Her determination and will to persevere have served Millie well; in fact, she continues to find success in her work. She now focuses her attention on helping other women achieve success. Whenever new women come to work at the plant, Millie coaches them. "I would tell other women to decide in their mind what they want to do, stick to it, and do it. You know, you see another person do it, you can do it too." She also tells other women that they have to find their own "technique" to be successful. In her own early work at the tire plant, Millie said that while others may do the work better or not as well, that she was determined and "set out to *do* it." In addition, she said that some supervisors may try and intimidate women workers, but that "once you let them know one time that you won't be pushed around, then you kind of got it knocked." As she stated in the interview, Millie and her co- workers are "leaning to whatever hope we have." That hope is found in the union. Millie is able to negotiate the conditions of her work in a male-dominated field through her experiences in the USWA.

Millie's attitude and strength are also derived from her experiences working at a non-union filter plant. She said that at the filter plant, a worker "had to fend for [herself]." Millie stated that position and advancement were based on "who [a person] knew." Workers did well based on "how [they] fit in with the crowd." A worker could lose a dispute based on whether managers "liked [a person] or if the supervisor was good friends with different workers." When she was laid off from the filter plant, Millie also lost her seniority, and she chose to find new work at the tire plant. At the union company, Millie did not fear favoritism or other unfair practices. Though she learned much of her feminism from her experiences in the union, she also developed an active feminist consciousness because of her mother's response to a patriarchal system. Millie reported that she learned a great deal from her mother's powerful example when she defied conventions to become a minister in a male-dominated profession. "She pastors a church and she's a woman. And coming up, I remember a lot of men saying that women weren't supposed to minister or anything like that. I remember that. And it never fazed her a bit. She done exactly what she believed in, and she went on from there." Her mother's determination to overcome gender discrimination together with Millie's own work experiences led her to develop a strong union feminist perspective.

Women's Union Leadership

In addition to advocating equity in work roles and responsibilities, union feminism incorporates new ideas about leadership and democracy. According to Bruce Kokopeli and George Lakey in *Leadership for Change: A Feminist Model*, "Feminist writers, social scientists and movement experimenters all point to new possibilities. The feminist perspective shows how old leadership models are intertwined with the continuation of patriarchy."[32] Union feminists are exploring avenues for dismantling the patriarchal agenda. For example, during her career in the USWA, Millie has assumed several leadership roles in her local and central union councils. As a member of the local executive board, she says, "I get to vote and make—help make—some of the decisions for the union." Her feminism extends to a call for representation and leadership in the male-dominated union. "I want to be in the decision-making. I ran last term and I managed to get it. [There were] nine men and one female, which was me, and I got it." It should be noted that in Millie's local there are 113 women out of 1100 members. In a union local with ten percent women, it is a testimony to the members' respect for and admiration of Millie's capabilities, irrespective of gender. For Millie, serving in a leadership position enables her to gain first-hand knowledge of situations that affect workers. She says, "I'm one, I like to know *up front*. I like to hear firsthand what's going on." Unions have provided the means for women to resist the sexism in their trades, offering influential roles to them. Currently Millie is working to develop greater involvement among women and to address their needs in the union. "We have a Silver Lights committee, we have a welfare committee, we have a Women of Steel [group]. You know, just that women can come together and voice their opinion on what's going on." She further reports that "women'll get stuff done. On this committee, we want to assist all the other committees. We are trying to help [women] get active and trying to make the local better." Her own work in the union has enabled her to grow politically and to gain new leadership abilities. Millie continues to hone her skills. In fact, at the interview, she gave me a copy of the history of women's involvement in the USWA, which was presented at a leadership conference that she attended. Millie's union feminism is based on her realization that "we got important work to do for women and all workers."

KIM: GAINING KNOWLEDGE, HAVING POWER

Several of the women in this study are involved in union leadership, experiences that help them weave their union feminism. Their solidarity includes the variety of women's experiences in their unions. Kim, another steelworker employed in tire manufacturing, is working toward the same goals as Millie. As a young adult, Kim was forced to confront the realities of work and independence after she was divorced and had to raise four children on her own. Her experiences in the union have been pivotal in her development, and she credits the union with helping her gain the knowledge necessary to take care of herself and to help others as well. As a local union leader, Kim has undergone a feminist transformation during her years as a member of the USWA. She explains that before she began working in a union plant, she was woefully ignorant about the economic and political climate in which she found herself. Union information and activities raised Kim's consciousness about the issues. "All of a sudden, something happened to me, and I'm wondering, 'What's going on?' But now I know what's happening in politics, what's happening around the world. Even with different countries. They [the union] teach you a lot of things. But the women are doing more, and I think that's because now [the union is] more inclusive." As defined by Mary Belenky and her colleagues in *Women's Ways of Knowing,* Kim has become a "passionate knower," a person who has learned to use herself as an "instrument of understanding."[33] Passionate knowers "seek to stretch the outer boundaries of their consciousness—by making the unconscious conscious, by consulting and listening to the self, by voicing the unsaid, by listening to others and staying alert to all the undercurrents of life about them."[34] While she previously lacked these connections, now Kim says that she is more involved in politics with a new awareness of what is going on in the country and in the world. Prior to her union experience and training, she did not realize what was happening within companies and across borders. Now Kim hopes that all workers can gain the knowledge and skills that unions offer to women. "I just wish every company would have a union. I do. I listen to some people talk about the way their supervisors talk to them or have let them go and don't have to have an explanation and don't warn them or don't tell them. I just wish everybody could have a union."

With the realization that unions empower workers, Kim hopes to widen the net to include all of her sisters and brothers in the plant.

Prior to working in a union environment, Kim did not understand how the USWA could benefit her. After the first strike, her father encouraged and educated her: "But my dad said, 'Yeah, you can afford to [cross the picket line] now, but if you don't go [out on strike] now, you won't be able to afford to live later.' Which I didn't understand, but I didn't go to work." The first strike is short-lived, but through this experience Kim began to see the power of the union to help her gain the knowledge and competence to take care of herself and her family. The first lesson was that while the union would help her and other workers, it was essential for unionists to be involved. Since knowledge is the key to her happiness and success, Kim has used her union experiences to gain the skills and insights she needed. She related her first awakening to this knowledge:

> I didn't even know that jobs like this existed, where you didn't have to do unsafe stuff. If you were going to stay late, they needed to give you notice, and so this was kind of new for me. But I'm one of them people, I got the need to know, so I figure if I'm in this union, I need to find out something about it. So I started going to the union meetings, and I felt like if I didn't like what was going on, I needed to get involved.

Previous economic threats to her survival were dire, but with her union experiences, Kim learned that she can make it on her own. However, she also wants to contribute her time and efforts to help other women and men who may have the same needs she once had. Kim is indeed a "need-to-know" person who uses her growing wisdom to empower others.

Solidarity and Social Justice

The second strike that occurred fifteen years after the initial dispute provides Kim with valuable knowledge and a solidarity standpoint. In describing the latter conflict, she related that the company inadvertently helped the union galvanize the membership into a stronger community of workers. The company's public attack on the workers' abilities and competence led to greater union participation.

> So we went on strike. This time it was different because the strike wouldn't have been, I don't think it would have turned so ugly if [they hadn't denigrated the workers]. The company helped us a lot. What they did was they started doing articles—they put articles in the [newspaper], and they were saying that half the people in here don't have

high school educations. It was like they were saying that a lot of them
were illiterate, and they should just be happy to have the money that
they are making.

The education that Kim and her fellow workers receive is not a formal,
traditional schooling experience; rather they are educated by working and
learning through the political and personal lessons of involvement in the
union. All of the furor surrounding the company's smear campaign against
the workers leads to what Kim describes as a "solid" union, made possible because of the public defamation of the workers. In a similar way, the
press shaped public opinion about the hundreds of women workers during
the 1909 Shirtwaist Strike in New York City. According to Nan Enstad in
Ladies of Labor, Girls of Adventure, "If public opinion deemed the striking
women to be legitimate political actors with grievances, owners would be
greatly pressured to bow to union demands or risk losing sales."[35] Therefore in that conflict, as well as in the tire workers strike, the company and
the media worked together to defame the workers and diminish their claims
against the company.

The solidarity of her fellow and sister workers and Kim's growing
involvement with the union converged during the 1999 strike. This labor
dispute lasted a year, eventually yielding major gains for union members
amid bitter negotiations and acrimony toward replacement workers. The
striking workers joined union members' actions around the world to fight
the company's injustice and greed. "We did a lot of things. We went to different plants that [the company] had, like they had a brake and suspension
plant, and we'd go there and we'd picket. And we would picket and tell
the people why we went out on strike. And the different stores, Ford and
places; they didn't want us in front of their stores." The organization and
implementation of these political strategies in the international steelworkers union demonstrate the extent of knowledge, competence, and solidarity
to empower individuals and the collective-subjective, in this case, the workers at the tire manufacturing plant.

During the strike, Kim and her co-workers found other temporary
jobs and worked for the union at the strike headquarters and on the picket
line during their off-hours. At her "temp" job, Kim discovered what working at a non-union plant means for the majority of North Carolina workers without representation and protection from corporate greed. Eventually
she was employed full time and worked for five months at a radiator company. While there, Kim was shocked to discover that the plant management secretly had been planning to close the facility. The managers of this
non-union company announced the news at a called meeting of employees

only two hours prior to the closure. Kim spoke out at the meeting, challenging the company's poor decision-making and lack of communication with workers.

> If they had time to draw up the checks and contact the unemployment office, they had plenty of time [to tell workers]. And I'm in this meeting, and I'm listening, and I just laugh, I don't believe this, which it doesn't really matter to me. And I spoke up, "You come in here telling people who been working here ten or twelve years, and this is two o'clock?" That's why I remember the time. "And it's two o'clock and at four o'clock, you tell people that they [will] no longer have a job?" I said, "I don't believe this." It was just ridiculous. I just could not believe this. But then after that, I was laid off, and I got unemployment. So then I really got to work on the strike then.

This negative example enabled Kim to recognize the plight of non-union workers who lack the knowledge and skills that union membership and advocacy provide.

In subsequent years, Kim has become an active union organizer and educator. Since her parents are deceased and her children are grown, the union has become her family. During the strike, this involvement with her newfound and extensive family—including overseas "relatives" in the international union—became even more important. "We were on the picket line, somebody was on the picket line all the time, we made sure somebody was there all the time, even in the cold, somebody was there all the time. because they had put up this little hut like thing. And I think everybody considered it home by then, cause then they were really 'cooking' [involved] in there." The union "home" and her new "family" gave Kim the support and care she needed so that she could in turn nurture and encourage others. She spoke of the work of her international union: "Now, when there's a strike, or we know somebody's having a strike, or somebody's trying to organize, we try to back them and help them, cause it helps to have somebody just to stop by, you know." Other local union organizations offered support to the striking tire workers. "Other unions like the machinists, the CWA, all the unions came in. They always brought something." The other union members' solidarity also extended beyond strike relief. As Kim says, "Any company that had a union would not deliver anything to the plant. One time, some of the [union] officers went out and stopped a train that brought stuff in and told them we were on strike. They wouldn't bring the stuff in. They took it all the way back." In addition, political leaders, including Senator John Edwards and Congressman Mel Watt, offered their support by visiting striking workers on the picket line. The USWA family of unionists expanded their kinship to other local unions and legislators, discovering the power of coalition-building efforts.

While the union is like a family for her, Kim also employs the metaphor of a church to describe union membership and participation. She uses this idea whenever she talks with prospective members, attempting to raise their consciousness. When she meets with new employees, Kim invites them to join the union, educating them in a language they can understand—one of belonging to a faith community. Kim realizes that, just as she was once, these workers "just don't know" what union membership can mean to a worker.

> Because just like the CEOs, they go to a company, they negotiate their salary, they negotiate their vacations, their benefits, their pensions, they negotiate all that. So I say, "That's us, we're negotiating what we want. But we're paying somebody to look out for *our* interests." That's how I explained it to them, and I say, "If you were in this church, and you were part of the seventy people that had to pay for the air conditioning, and lights and stuff, and you had thirty people who said that they are not, and they didn't, but when the lights and air conditioning come back on, they are standing in their part of the church and enjoying it, and, you know, just like you are, you are not gonna feel like that's fair, and that's how people feel." So when I'm talking to them when they first come in, that's when I tell them, try to [talk] so they will understand.

Whenever she encounters individuals who are reluctant to join the union, Kim is not frustrated. Rather, she considers the injustices against workers and the ignorance of most southern workers regarding unions and their rights. Then she seeks to educate them—to help them—as she herself once was helped by her father and other unionists. As Maxine Greene suggests,

> There have been those who saw the relation between participation and individual development, between finding one's voice and creating a self in the midst of other selves. There have been those who have named the obstacle to their own becoming in self-regard, in indifference, in lack of mutuality and care. How, in a society like ours, a society of contesting interests and submerged voices, an individualist society, a society still lacking an "in-between," can we educate for freedom? And, in educating for freedom, how can we create and maintain a common world?[36]

Many women find their freedom in a labor union. However, the process of education is essential for women to find their voices and to create common ground in union feminism. According to Lorraine Masterson in "Feminist Leaders Can't Walk on Water," women leaders must emphasize education. "If we as women are working to create a world in which power and responsibility are shared by all people, then we must understand the process by which people become leaders, and thereby lead ourselves and each other toward that goal."[37] A 2003 American Association of University Women report, *Global Voices for Gender Equity*, echoes this idea: building on women's knowledge and educating them "in power" leads to improved conditions and social justice.[38] As a union feminist leader, Kim empowers herself and others to achieve greater understanding and action.

"Doing the Politics"

Because of the extensive knowledge that Kim has gained through her work with the union—locally, nationally, and internationally—she understands the political implications of her work. "The union teaches you a lot." However, this knowledge often depresses her. "Sometimes it's kind of depressing, especially when you know what's going on in the Congress and with the politicians. It's kind of depressing, but then it makes you work harder cause you try to make people understand." She adds, "It kind of makes you feel sad because you wish you could do more." Her political activism, born of her own struggles as single mother, trying to raise her children with positive values, keeps her strong and laboring for the cause. She states, "I just wish everyone could have a union." The union may be a family substitute for Kim, but it is also the place where her politics is situated. As she says, "I do the politics." Later in her narrative, Kim talks about the role of women in the union, admitting how hard it is for women to find the time to work for the cause. "I can understand because they have families and stuff like that, but I think once a woman starts to work in a union, then she kind of gets passionate about it." This passion for family, solidarity, justice, and independence all combine to make Kim a powerful advocate for the union and for all working people, emerging in a union feminism that extends to educate and unite other working-class women and men.

ELLEN: TRANSFORMATIVE UNION FEMINISM

Ellen is another respondent in this study who serves as an active union feminist. A thirty-one-year veteran of the telecommunications industry, she faced harassment and discrimination at various times during her career. Ellen's experiences include work in the female-dominated operator section, clerical work for male supervisors, and an outside job as a technician in service and repair. Eventually she moved into what is also considered a "man's" job, as an underground cable splicing technician. She said, "That was the best job I ever had. And I stayed there until I retired." She was one of two women in that role. "I was the second woman to have ever been in that work group, and I was one of two in that work center." According to Ellen, women began pursuing the outside jobs because of lost positions in other areas when call centers were consolidated or when jobs were eliminated. In addition, the outside, "men's," jobs paid more, attracting greater numbers of women. As Ellen reported, "The women's jobs don't pay as much as the outside jobs, so we started going outside." She told of dealing with sexism in this new area of work for her. "There was one guy in my group who told me to my face he didn't want to work with me." Ellen noted that all women had to prove their capabilities in the repair jobs. She recalled a time when she worked for the cable repair section. "You have to prove yourself, you know, and I just wanted to get my hands in it and see what I could do with the job." She said that the work was hard even without "trying to work with a bunch of testosterone men." However, Ellen was skilled at her job, stating that she eventually earned the respect of the men in her work group.

One reason women have difficulty proving themselves on the job is that work groups and departments can either be fractured and uncaring or they may be such a unified bloc that women workers are unable penetrate the barrier. When she worked in installation and repair, Ellen said that the men had not "bonded," stating that they "didn't want to help anybody. They didn't help each other at all." However, when she went to work with the cable group, it was a different environment. These men had solidarity and supported one another, often to the exclusion of a newcomer. She says, "It was all for one, one for all. If you didn't do what the rest of them did, you were an outcast." Though the cable crew was a unified team, they still resented having to work with a woman. Ellen stated, "You have to prove yourself, you know." In fact, when she first went out with a crew of men to work in cable repair, Ellen was forced, as the "low man on the totem pole," to do the hardest, dirtiest work. When her partner left her alone at a work site to do heavy lifting and a complicated setup on her own, Ellen did it. She had been taught some short-cuts and strategies to deal with heavy, difficult work by an "old-school" trainer. "So I got out and set up the hole just like I was just going to go ahead and do this, you know. And when he came [to the work site], he was really shocked. And when he went back [to the crew's work center], he told them, 'She set that hole up all by herself, you know. She's okay.' So then any time he was sent to work with me, he goes, 'Okay.'" Though she was grudgingly accepted by most of the crew, Ellen often faced obstacles because of gender inequality throughout her career.

One of Ellen's first roles in the company led to a showdown with a supervisor who treated her unfairly. She said that she had not desired a transfer to this urban job, but she had no choice since the call center closed in the mountain town where she had previously worked. "I really didn't want to go to Charlotte to begin with, but I ended up in motor vehicles. And this boss was like the boss from hell. He didn't like work to begin with, and he would kind of overburden you with whatever he could come up with, things that you weren't supposed to do [ordinarily]." In addition to being treated unfairly, Ellen was also isolated from co-workers. "My office was way back off in the back, and I didn't have any contact with anybody during the day." Since much of the work assigned to her was not "in her job description," Ellen consulted with her union representative about what she should do. She said, "I was making arrangements for his *golf* outings." The union president told her to return the inappropriate work to her supervisor and to tell him that she was not going to complete it.

> So he walked in one day with a stack of papers about this high, and he said, "You need to go through these for me and break them up and file them where they're supposed to be filed." And before he could lay them down, I said, "Well, that really isn't part of my job." And he took [the papers] and tossed them in my lap across the desk and hit me in stomach with them and said, "It's your job now." And so I picked up the papers, and I tossed them back at him, which he didn't catch them, and they went in the floor. And I said, "Now you need to give them back to whoever they hit before me." Because we were at a mutual standoff there.

Ellen did not pick up the papers, and when her supervisor returned, he said that he was going to suspend her. She told him: "If you want to suspend me for not doing somebody else's work, you can do that, but I really feel that you're being unfair to me." Her supervisor gave her an ultimatum: either to have the papers picked up by the time he returned or to leave. As soon as he left the room, Ellen called the personnel office to arrange a transfer. When her supervisor came back, he wrote her up for insubordination, and Ellen called her union president to file a grievance in the case.

At her grievance hearing, both the union president and the supervisor effectively silenced Ellen with their abusive verbal sparring. As Ellen recounted, the union president was very aggressive, not like the typical "southern president" that the supervisor was accustomed to; "he was like the one you read about from up North somewhere." The union president arrived at the meeting smoking a cigar and wearing bedroom slippers. Ellen described the following exchange:

> [The union president] sits down across the desk from this fellow, and says, "Now what are we here for?" And [the supervisor] said, "She was insubordinate." The union president said, "Well, you know, the little girl has been calling me about you giving her all this extra work. It's really not fair for you to do this. If you think just because she is from the mountains, she's stupid, well, she's not. You really shouldn't be doing this." [The supervisor] said, "Well, I just wanted to train her differently. I wanted her to be a real clerk." So then the president starts yelling all this profanity and calls him the sorriest SOB that ever walked the face of the earth.

At this point, Ellen thought, "I'm fired. I am just absolutely fired." Ellen was not allowed to represent herself at the meeting though she later won the grievance and eventually left that job. However, as with other times in her work, she had to fight for her rights, all of which led to her union feminist perspective.

Ellen also recounted her work in another office for a male supervisor who "hated women. In fact, he hated his wife. He must have had twelve [wives] in the time I knew him." Though she arrived at the first meeting with this new supervisor as a union representative, the man treated her as a subordinate merely because she was a woman, asking her to prepare coffee for everyone at the meeting.

> And so, you know I didn't make any coffee. I just sat down. And he turned around and said, "Didn't you hear me?" And I said, "Yes, I heard you, but you obviously are mistaken if you think I'm making coffee." So, you know, he was beside himself. So when we went in the meeting, he was just, it actually threw him off that a female was there. It was the start of the meeting, kind of set the tone for it, you know. "The coffee's there, girl." You could tell what kind of guy he was.

The sexism and discrimination that Ellen repeatedly faced in her early career only served to fuel her union feminism. However, Ellen's own work experiences were not the only ones that led to her fight for social justice.

"Norma Rae" Redux

Early in her career, Ellen served as a United Way volunteer, going to various companies to talk with their workers. From these experiences, she gained insights into the ways that unions help empower women workers. At one site in particular, an Asheville shirt factory, Ellen noted that the workers— all women—were subjected to oppressive conditions. The factory manager told Ellen that he would approve the United Way presentation only if it was scheduled during the workers' lunch break. He said that the workers "get thirty minutes for lunch, and they'll be eating lunch while you're talking to them." After her presentation, *all* of the women donated to the charity, and many of them gave their "fair share," one hour's pay per month. When Ellen looked at their donation cards, she had difficulty understanding the amounts donated. She asked the personnel manager who was assisting her if the donations had been calculated correctly. Ellen could not believe their low wages. "They make so little, and here they are giving that much." At that moment the factory manager arrived in time to hear Ellen say, "How do they make any money?" The personnel manager told her that they made their wages by "piece work," or production premiums. "And so [the factory manager] tapped me on the shoulder and said, 'I don't need no 'Norma Rae' in here. I think you can leave now.'" Years later, Ellen continues to be outraged by the conditions in that factory.

> I just can't believe this is right that these women make this amount of money, because to me, these women all had families. How in the world could they survive? And to make them take thirty minutes for lunch and make them listen to the United Way? And he didn't even pay them for the thirty minutes, for the United Way presentation. For the life of me, I couldn't understand how this man who worked these women like dogs could possibly treat them this way. I was so used to being treated fair at all times because I had worked for a union company.

Ellen had seen the benefits, particularly for women, of membership in a powerful national union. Another example of Ellen's social activism occurred when she worked with Raleigh sanitation workers, trying to organize a union for them. "We were organizing public workers here in Raleigh, and I started going to their grievance meetings with the workers. I had grievance training and leadership training through the CWA [Communication Workers of America]." City officials previously had been able to confuse the workers with complicated paperwork during the grievance process, so Ellen and her colleagues in the CWA helped the workers navigate the system. Their organizing effort ultimately failed, however, because of the low wages of the workers. "It's hard to get them to sign a union card because they have to pay their dues at the beginning. They're at a disadvantage. They don't make a lot [of money]. They do need representation though." Ellen continues to work on the behalf of unorganized and oppressed workers.

The path to Ellen's empowerment as a union feminist did not begin with her working life; rather it developed in her family of origin. She stated that her father was a "union man" and theirs was a union family. "My father was a union leader which was unusual because of where I come from [the mountains of North Carolina]." She told me that her father was a self-taught sheet metal worker who joined the union. "I was kind of raised knowing what a business agent was and going to union meetings. [My father] did take me to union meetings." Ellen was also a child who did not conform to the status quo. She tells of riding a segregated school bus where the African American children were forced to ride in the back. She says that the white children "would stand and hold the rails rather than go to the back of the bus to sit with the blacks." Ellen, who is white, failed to see the logic in this behavior. One day when there were no seats available, she sat with the African American children at the back of the bus. "Being the little rebel that I was, I go to the back of the bus and sit down. Well, when the bus driver looked in the rear view mirror and saw me in the back, he stopped the bus and told me to come up front." When she told him that she would get off at her stop, the driver was obliged to start the bus and continue his route. Ellen's mother disapproved of her daughter's violation of the social code, but her father applauded her effort though he cautioned her to avoid "upsetting" her mother if possible. However, her bold action on the bus changed the behavior of the other children. "I was the first one, and then after a while, it got to where we just sat wherever we wanted to on that particular bus." Ellen's courage, her "rebellion," led to positive social change even when she was a child.

Ellen also rebelled whenever an authority figure told her to do something for no apparent reason. She says, "I believed in doing what they told me to do, but there had to be a reason for it." As she says, she "broke the mold" in many ways, including playing with boys and defying her teacher's rule to write exclusively with her right hand though she was ambidextrous. One reason for her rebellious nature was that she had, as she says, an unreasonable, "overprotective" mother who did not want her to swim, ride a bicycle, or play with boys. Her father once said of Ellen, "You know, most people are going to fashion shows and little debutante balls, and my daughter, I have to go to a picket line or a union meeting to find her." Ellen says that she never wanted to be like her mother, rejecting the image that her mother represented: "a southern lady who never cussed, never drank, never did anything but what southern ladies do." She valued her father's world more. "My daddy went where he wanted to go, and he did what he wanted to do. He made his own money. My mother was dependent on my father. I never wanted to be dependent." Ellen's personal quest for freedom from "ladyhood" and a conventional life later led her to develop an independent spirit, which evolved into union feminism when she became an adult.

After high school, Ellen found the independence that she craved through work. She reported that she did not want to go to college; she wanted to work. However, her father insisted that she avoid working in a factory. "I don't know why he didn't want me to work in a factory, but he said, 'I don't want you to do plant work.' So the only other three companies were CP&L [Carolina Light and Power Company], Southern Bell, and Sears." Ellen completed applications at all three companies and talked it over with her father. "I said, 'You know, I can go to work for CP&L, and it's non-union, go to work for Sears, and it's non-union, or I can go work for Southern Bell, and it's union.' So I got in [Southern Bell] and went into operator services." As a union worker about to go on strike, Ellen took her cues from her father. "He told me to store up a lot of soup because we would get real hungry." When she was confronted with a "wildcat," or unsanctioned strike at her workplace, Ellen would not cross the picket line, even though she was later suspended for her actions. "I was suspended for my first wildcat because I was young and dumb and didn't know any better. And because I was raised in a union household, I knew that if you went to work and there were people walking outside [on a picket line] that you didn't go in." From the beginning of her career, Ellen knew that union membership meant activism and solidarity.

Ellen became a union leader in her years with the Communication Workers of America when most women did not get involved for various reasons. Ellen attributes her success in part to her early involvement with the Western North Carolina Central Labor Council. "I was offered opportunities that men were used to getting, but women weren't. [The council president] gave me my first opportunity to become involved in politics because he made me the volunteer political coordinator for the labor council. That opened up a whole lot of doors." While a man, the president of that group, had given her the opportunity, other men tried to take it away. In the union as well as on the job, Ellen faced discrimination when she tried to represent her local as a member of the labor council. Whenever she went to meetings as a delegate for the council, Ellen was told what to say and how to vote while previous male delegates had not been so advised. "Usually women were told what position they were going to take on certain issues. And before I left town, I knew how I was supposed to vote because it had kind of been given to me." When it came to endorsing a candidate for the United States Senate election, Ellen voted against what she had been advised. As she says, "God gave me a mind, and I'm going to have to use it. And I appreciate all the information that you can give me to help me make up my mind. But if there's an alternative route that's better, I'm going to take it." Even though she had not "followed orders," she says that she eventually won the council members' respect because she "had actually researched it and not just done it on a whim." In the face of this overt discounting of her intelligence, Ellen had the good fortune to meet the so-called "godfather of the union" in North Carolina, who empowered her to think for herself and to find her own voice. This man helped Ellen to gain the confidence and the skills to become a high-level leader in the union. In fact, upon her retirement from the company, Ellen has become an effective activist for labor issues in North Carolina.

A WORKING-CLASS FEMINIST AGENDA

Like Ellen's social justice activism on behalf of workers across the state, Kim as a member of the USWA, is working in the union environment to bring about a feminist awakening and increase the store of knowledge for active women. Kim says that her pro-union activities include doing "the politics." Women are "doing better" in the USWA, Kim acknowledges, with increased participation. "This was the first year we've ever had a woman district rep. We had a woman to run, and she got it and now we have an international women's conference, and that's good, you know, so they're doing better." She goes on to report that women currently are actively pursuing leadership roles.

> And now you meet more women presidents when we go to different conferences, you see more women presidents now, but not nearly enough. No, we had our women's conference, we had some real strong, good speakers; now that's something good. And [USWA] President Gerard was asking what did we think was wrong with the union, and this one lady stood up and she said, "Well, they're too male, too pale, and too stale!"

The increased participation in the union together with the knowledge gained during that involvement offer working-class women opportunities for growth and transformation as feminists. "They're more active now than they used to be, and I can understand it. I think once a woman starts to work in a union, then she kind of gets passionate about it, you know." Prior to her union experience, Kim notes that she "didn't pay any attention

to politics." Her new political awareness—together with her union activity—engenders a positive, powerful feminism.

The interpretive community, or subjective-collective, shared by these
women is one of working-class women in the South; therefore their feminism, when they claim it or exemplify it, necessarily reflects this perspective. Their feminism is evident in the women's language of self-reliance and
independence, the metaphors of church and family, and the ideals of pride
in one's work and proving oneself worthy. These characterize the collective-
subjective of working-class women in the twentieth-century South. While
these women speak to the power relations inherent in their lives, each
responds in individual ways. As Kathleen Casey points out in *I Answer
with My Life*: "[E]very study of narrative is based on a particular understanding of the speaker's self."[39] Therefore each of the women frames her
experiences in particular ways while retaining authority as an expert in her
life story. However, as part of an interpretive community, each also adopts
similar perspectives and patterns of priorities that reveal insights about the
working lives of North Carolina women during this period. The working-
class feminist consciousness that incorporates the lived experiences of the
women in this study emerges as union feminism.

According to Mary Margaret Fonow, union feminism is essentially
a fight for social justice for working-class women. "Union feminists
understood that it would be up to them to make their union understand that
women's rights were legitimate trade-union issues. To do so, they would
need the support of the emerging body of civil rights and human rights
law and the energy and forward momentum of the women's movement."[40]
The variety of women's experiences working in male-dominated industries
such as steel-making and telecommunications converge in a feminism that
protects their rights and includes the many cultures of women in the trades.
"Women steelworkers from different racial and cultural backgrounds and
from a variety of working-class occupations have been forging a unique
collective identity within their union as feminists and as trade unionists
during the past twenty-five years. They continue to do so at a time when
solidarity across lines of difference is more difficult to construct and
maintain."[41] Women such as Millie, Kim, and Ellen, who assume active
participation and leadership, learn that the union is the loom upon which
they may weave the unique tapestries of feminism that will serve them
and their sisters in the world of work. As Fonow notes, "Union resources
make it possible for working-class women, who would otherwise not
have the finances, to participate in the construction of union feminism."[42]
"Women of Steel," an effective education and empowerment program in
the USWA, provides women workers with the ways and means to connect

"the women's movement with the labor movement."[43] For Kim and Millie, active USWA participants, their union serves feminism in many aspects, providing resources and networks and ultimately mobilizing women to act on behalf of all women workers.

THE PROMISE OF UNION FEMINISM

Women who have been involved in labor disputes in North Carolina represent oppressed women in the South and around the world today. With the powerful new tool of union feminism, these women are resisting injustice, gender discrimination, sexual harassment, and economic oppression in their families, in their workplaces, in the corporate boardrooms, and in their unions. However, as Kim states, "[The union] let me know that you have to fight" even though, as she says, "you shouldn't have to fight, but you do when you work with companies like this." In a similar fashion, bell hooks calls for a radical change that may be realized with union feminism:

> Given the changing realities of class in our nation, widening gaps between the rich and poor, and the continued feminization of poverty, we desperately need a mass-based radical feminist movement that can build on the strength of the past, including the positive gains generated by reforms, while offering meaningful interrogation of existing feminist theory that was simply wrongminded while offering us new strategies. Significantly a visionary movement would ground its work in the concrete conditions of working-class and poor women. That means creating a movement that begins education for critical consciousness. . . . [44]

As Sally Miller Gearhart suggests in "The Future—If There Is One—Is Female," the "female future" consists of women and men claiming power and toppling patriarchal structures by employing traditional feminine characteristics such as "empathy, nurturance, and cooperation."[45] For the union feminist, power necessarily is constructed by equality, access, and involvement of all concerned parties. Dianne Balser echoes this idea.

> The fact that all women share a single gender identity and simultaneously are members of other oppressed groups is a source of both conflict and power. While these differences between women can and do precipitate conflicts, each group of women also adds a unique perspective and richness to the total understanding of the female experience. Most important, women have access to every other oppression. Thus women cannot really end their own oppression without ending the

oppression of all other peoples. Likewise every other oppressed group must tackle sexism in order to be liberated.[46]

Union feminism incorporates the multiple perspectives of different affinity groups, creating effective and powerful coalitions that value differences and attend to the struggles of all oppressed people. The union feminist effort continues in the work of thousands of women in the South and around the world who are fighting oppression, social injustice, and poverty in local and global contexts.

Chapter Seven

Global Solidarity:
The Warp and Weft of Change

Job losses, global markets, and anti-union efforts affect the lives of women in this study and the experiences of women workers around the world. Global solidarity is woven in the fabric of strong international unions, providing an effective antidote to corporate greed and oppression. Much has been written about the loss of manufacturing jobs in the United States, and industries in North Carolina have not been spared. Since the implementation of the North American Free Trade Agreement (NAFTA), more than 2.7 million manufacturing jobs across the country have been lost.[1] In the South, workers in the textile industry in particular have been affected by economic globalization. In this one major industry, job losses and plant closings have devastated entire communities. In 2003, 78 percent of all textile jobs in the United States were located in the South, and in North Carolina, more than 2700 textile jobs were lost in the fourth quarter of 2001 alone.[2] Manufacturing jobs continue to disappear rapidly. Since the advent of NAFTA, more than 16,000 textile jobs in North Carolina were lost between December 2000 and March 2002.[3] Economic globalization has taken a toll on the working class, leaving many workers to seek retraining for service and technical jobs, most of which offer only a fraction of the wages and benefits that were available in manufacturing jobs. No simple solution will address these problems. The crisis of globalization reflects a complex series of long-term, ongoing events that affect the working lives of people everywhere on the planet.

Thriving international economies are influencing both minor and substantial changes in jobs, finances, and union membership. As David Korten notes in his 2001 study, *When Corporations Rule the World,*

> The past two decades have seen the most rapid and sweeping institutional transformation in human history. It is a conscious and intentional

transformation in search of a new world economic order in which business has no nationality and knows no borders. It is driven by global
dreams of vast corporate empires, compliant governments, a globalized
consumer monoculture, and a universal ideological commitment to corporate libertarianism.[4]

Korten describes corporate libertarians as the self-proclaimed gurus of
the so-called "free" trade, "free" market economies that claim to support
improved wealth and sustainability on a global level. However, in reality,
these corporate libertarians are leveraging increasingly lax government regulations to their advantage. Korten states, "Through deregulation and the
removal of national economic borders we have created a global economy
more powerful than any national government."[5] Capital becomes king;
the wealthy become wealthier; and as jobs are created in poorer countries,
neither the workers nor their governments become enriched. Rather they
subject their workers to dangerous, inhumane conditions for starvation
wages. The only winners in the globalization game are upper echelon executives and company stockholders, and the crisis is worsening. According
to Korten, "[C]orporate globalization is enriching the few at the expense
of the many, replacing democracy with rule by corporations and financial
elites, destroying the real wealth of the planet and society to make money
for the already wealthy, and eroding the relationships of trust and caring
that are the essential foundation of a civilized society."[6] These phenomena
are reflected in the dramatic changes in manufacturing jobs in North Carolina.

GLOBALIZATION AND WOMEN WORKERS IN NORTH CAROLINA

The women in this study have been variably affected by globalization
though the movements of labor and capital have had some impact on all of
them. For example, the older women I interviewed who worked in the textile industry in the first half of the twentieth century had access to those jobs
because of the migration of the textile industry from the North to the South
between 1890 and 1920. Annie is just one of the respondents in this project
whose work was made possible by the migration of textile jobs. Annie was
a "scab," or replacement worker, during the General Textile Strike of 1934,
a nationwide effort that resulted in long-lasting consequences for workers in the South. Another respondent, Katherine, participated in a bloody
conflict in 1958 in her small textile-dependent town in northeastern North
Carolina. Both of these women and hundreds of thousands of other textile

workers in the state owed their jobs to the textile industry's migration south in the aftermath of the southern Reconstruction and increasing unionization of northern industries. The problem of capital migration, in pursuit of low-wage employees and non-union workers, is one that is being replicated across the globe in the present day. Yesterday's job losses across the nation parallel today's job losses around the globe. However, neither Annie nor Katherine would consider these larger forces as being responsible for their work, their livelihoods, and their union experiences. According to Jacquelyn Hall and her colleagues in *Like a Family: The Making of a Southern Cotton Mill World*, the labor problems of modern globalization and manufacturing are mirrored in the lives of the early textile workers.

> Southern manufacturers could pay less because they purchased labor in a regional market where the general level of economic development kept wages low. Lower labor costs, in turn, made southern products more competitive in national and international markets, and mill owners, rather than workers, reaped the rewards. From the outset, textile entrepreneurs realized generous returns on their investments. "It was not unusual for mills in [the early] years . . . to make 30 per cent to 75 per cent profit."[7]

Hall and her colleagues detail the pandemic of health hazards, deplorable working conditions, and low wages for southern workers, all of which are being repeated around the globe today.

THE RISE OF THE MAQUILADORAS

Though writing about workers in the early to mid-twentieth century South, Hall and her fellow researchers could well be reporting about life in 2004 in the *maquiladoras*, which are manufacturing facilities in the free trade zones in Mexico. The maquiladoras are industrial sites where hundreds of thousands of workers live in unsanitary, unsafe, makeshift shacks with little or no water or sanitary facilities. They work long hours in dangerous conditions for little pay. Their number is increasing dramatically with each new year and with every new relaxed trade agreement. "Growth has been explosive, from 620 maquiladora plants employing 119,500 workers in 1980 to 2,200 factories employing more than 500,000 workers in 1992."[8] Like those of their sisters and brothers in the southeastern United States a century earlier when jobs migrated South, the wages of workers in the maquiladoras undercut the pay of other workers around the globe. Workers in the maquiladoras average $1.64 an hour, compared to an average of $16.17 an hour for U.S. workers in manufacturing.[9] In addition, environmental regulations are either nonexistent or ignored, and toxic dumping is common. "Mexican workers, including children, are heroes of the new economic order in the eyes of the corporate libertarians—sacrificing their health, lives, and futures on the altar of global competition."[10] Naomi Klein's research confirms Korten's findings. In her 2002 expose, *No Logo*, Klein explores the effects of what she calls the "discarded factory" on women in the work world: "Today's 'new deal' with workers is a non-deal; one-time manufacturers, turned marketing mavens, are so resolutely intent on evading any and all commitments that they are creating a workforce of childless women [in the maquiladoras], a system of footloose factories employing footloose workers."[11] Profits for the already wealthy few influenced the southern migration of textile and other manufacturing jobs in the past and continue to push the relentless, rapacious agenda of modern capitalists—all achieved at the expense of the workers.

UNION ANTIDOTES TO GREED

For most of the working women in this study, labor unions have been an effective antidote to the diseased capitalism of corporate libertarians. In particular, the textile, paper, and furniture industries in North Carolina have been the most adversely affected by the globalization of capital and labor. Job losses and decline in union membership are greatest in the textile industry. As a former textile employee, Joan is the only respondent in this study who currently is a union member. Joan's narrative shares her experiences during a strike in 1988. The plant where she worked manufactured exclusive lingerie, employing mostly women for the specialized sewing of expensive women's undergarments. When their contract was submitted for renewal, the owner's son, who had only recently become CEO, did not, as Joan says, "bargain in good faith" with the workers. The CEO wanted to slash workers' retirement and health care benefits while increasing their work hours from thirty-five to forty per week. While globalization was not the only factor in the altered working conditions and the unwillingness of management to bargain, corporate greed and union busting tactics led to the workers' strike, which lasted nearly a year. When the negotiations were complete and the strike ended, Joan attempted to lead workers through the new contract, but faced increasing hostility from the company officials since she was the spokesperson and leader of the strike. After months of harassment and fighting for workers' rights, Joan accepted a position with the union, becoming a business agent with the company. The company ultimately consolidated its industry into one plant in the northeastern United

States. Joan's plant has since closed, perhaps directly or indirectly because of the strike and the quest for lower wages and higher profits for executives and stockholders. This type of union-busting has increased dramatically since the passage of NAFTA. According to Naomi Klein:

> In North America and Europe, job flight is a threat with which workers have become all too familiar. A study commissioned by the NAFTA labor commission found that in the United States, between 1993 and 1995, employers threatened to close the plant in 50 percent of the all union certification elections. . . . Specific, unambiguous threats ranged from attaching shipping labels to equipment throughout the plant with a Mexican address, to posting maps of North America with an arrow pointing from the current plant site to Mexico. The study found that the employers followed through on the threats, shutting down all or part of newly unionized plants, in 15 percent of these cases—triple the closing rate of the pre-NAFTA 1980s.[12]

Klein points out that workers in other countries are not protected from job migration either. Whenever and wherever workers attempt to organize, the jobs take flight again. Unions are also weakened by recent company policy changes and an economic downturn since 2001. In 1973, more than 24 percent of employees in the United States were union workers; in 2000, fewer than 14 percent were union workers.[13] By 2004, that number had decreased to 12.5 percent.[14] And as Barbara Ehrenreich notes in *Nickel and Dimed: On (Not) Getting By in America*, the "AFL-CIO estimates that ten thousand workers a year are fired for participating in union organizing drives."[15]

For five workers in this study, the closing of the Ecusta Paper Corporation, a manufacturing facility in Transylvania County, North Carolina, reflects a microcosm of union-busting and globalization during the twentieth century. In the 1930s, Harry H. Straus, a paper manufacturer and entrepreneur from Germany emigrated to the United States, settling first in New York and later relocating to western North Carolina where he created the Ecusta Paper Company. Prior to the development of the large-scale cigarette-paper manufacturing plant, Transylvania County's two main industries were pulpwood production, involving clear-cutting timber, and tanneries, which prepares animal hides for various human uses. In 1939, more than 900 workers were hired at the Ecusta mill. Within five years, more than 2,000 employees had been hired, and at its peak, Ecusta employed nearly 3,000 people[16] When Straus built Ecusta, he instituted a program of welfare capitalism. He built the county's first health care facilities on the plant site, created recreation and cultural activities for workers, and improved the standard of living for everyone in Transylvania County. Straus's successful empire lasted nearly ten years before Ecusta was purchased by Olin Industries, an affiliate of corporate cellophane giant, DuPont. During this time workers enjoyed good wages and fair working conditions. When the company again was sold, Ecusta workers faced wage losses, a decline in benefits, and lack of representation. They later organized with the Paper, Allied-Industrial, Chemical, and Energy Workers International Union (PACE).

As a unionized workforce, workers maintained their relatively high standards of living through several subsequent corporate incarnations. However, when the company was sold to a transnational corporation early in 2001, the new owner, a British citizen named Nathu Puri, initially promised stability and continued progress at Ecusta. However, Puri's real agenda was different. He began to request a "raft of givebacks" from workers, "starting with a 25 percent wage cut."[17] He also demanded a "tripling of employee self-payment for health insurance, elimination of retiree health insurance and paid holidays, a major cut in Sunday premium pay, and the end of contract language protecting the workers' jobs if the plant is sold."[18] When the union negotiations for a new labor agreement ultimately failed, and the workers went on strike, Puri closed the plant. This closure, representing more than 1200 lost jobs, devastated the people in the plant as well as those in the county who were economically dependent on Ecusta wages and tax revenues.

"THOSE RICH BASTARDS"

As shown in chapter four, the corporate greed exemplified by the Ecusta debacle deeply affected Stella, a respondent in this study who worked for the company for forty-nine years before her retirement. Stella explained that all workers, even the salaried employees, are protected by unions, and workers who are not members of unions suffer. "My grandfather worked at the Carr Lumber Company where they gave workers just enough money to live on. This was a result of not having a union." Stella went on to tell the story of how railroad magnate George Vanderbilt gained control of what later became the Pisgah National Forest, indicating that he "stole one hundred acres that my grandfather had bought for $30 in the Pisgah Forest. [Vanderbilt's] another one of those rich bastards who made money off the poor people." Stella's "Big-Me-and-the-Little-You Concept" reflects her ideas about wealth and the working class. She also noted that individuals who oppose organized labor are "stupid people against unions [who] just help rich people drain poor people of their life." This is true in Transylvania County where the loss of the Ecusta jobs threatens the well-being of nearly all citizens who reside in the community. Stella further stated that "most of the business people in this town hate the union." When I asked her why that was so, she emphatically stated, "*Total, unadulterated ignorance.*" Stella used her salary to explain her point: "I started out in '51 making $1.09 an hour. When I finished Ecusta in 1999, I was making almost $19 an hour. But that was because of the union."

SOUTHERN ANTI-UNION SENTIMENT

Anti-union sentiments in Transylvania County reflect the views of many people in the South. This attitude persists in part because of the failures of the General Textile Strike of 1934, losses that continue to echo in the memories of those who lived through it and in the imaginations of their descendants. In 1934 striking workers endured bloody battles with mill owners and their enforcers, local and state governments whose police forces quelled the "rebellion." In the documentary film, *The Uprising of '34*, Joe Jacobs tells his story. "It was on Labor Day 1934 that I witnessed the closest thing that this country has had to a revolution. The General Textile Strike was one of the largest strikes in American history, it was the culmination of years of home-grown organizing and protest. For many Southern workers it was the first time they had raised their voices as citizens to challenge the control of the mill owners."[19] Because of the trauma that the workers and their families experienced during this cataclysmic labor dispute, today many people will not talk about or consider labor unions. Flora Maye Caldwell, also interviewed in the film, notes that "nobody will talk about it and—only to say, 'I will not be a part of this union because of what happened long ago.'"[20] Lori Rushmeyer expressed the thinking of many people after the General Textile Strike of 1934. "At one time I tried to talk to my father about [a] union and he told me, he says, 'Well, at one time there was a union, and they came in and they took the money from the people and they left them high and dry.'"[21] Union organizers argue that they could not possibly have taken care of 500,000 striking workers across the country. Joe Jacobs explains:

> This was a revolution of five hundred thousand people. How do you feed five hundred thousand people? How do you find houses for five hundred thousand people? We couldn't overcome it. That's why I get

so mad when they say that we walked off and left 'em. We sweated blood trying to take care of them. We couldn't. And the people who suffered, instead of being mad at the boss because he wouldn't take him back, the propaganda was you see what happened: the union got you out on strike and now they walked off and left you.[22]

People all across the South who have had little experience with labor unions believed this anti-union propaganda and often blocked organizing efforts out of, as Stella stated, "total, unadulterated ignorance."

Modern Union-Busting Tactics

In the present day, anti-union propaganda serves to support long-held views against organizing efforts in the South; however, major corporations around the globe are also making concerted efforts to prevent unionization. In *Nickel and Dimed*, Barbara Ehrenreich writes about how retail giant Wal-Mart's vigorous anti-union screed is presented to new workers via a series of training videos. "'[V]arious associates testify to the essential feeling of family for which Wal-Mart is so well-known,' leading up to the conclusion that we don't need a union."[23] In the videos, unions are attacked for causing job losses and are depicted as self-serving only to get dues from hard-working people. In addition, a Wal-Mart video suggests, "you would lose 'your voice' because the union would insist on doing your talking for you. Finally, you might even lose your wages and benefits because they would all be 'at risk on the bargaining table.'"[24] The union-busting tactics known to Wal-Mart employees are replicated on an international scale.

Naomi Klein notes that when, "in the late eighties, Korean workers began to rebel against their dollar-a-day wages and formed trade unions to fight for better conditions," the companies took their jobs to yet another country, outsourcing higher wage work to lower wage countries.[25] "The transience woven into the fabric of free-trade zones is an extreme manifestation of the corporate divestment of the world of work, which is taking place at all levels of industry."[26] Traditional unions have little hope of organizing transient workers, yet an international union would support all workers in ways that the fragmented unions in the developed nations and non-unionized countries cannot. As the Industrial Workers of the World state in their preamble,

> We find that the centering of the management of industries into fewer and fewer hands makes the trade unions unable to cope with the ever growing power of the employing class. The trade unions fos-

ter a state of affairs which allows one set of workers to be pitted against another set of workers in the same industry, thereby helping defeat one another in wage wars. Moreover, the trade unions aid the employing class to mislead the workers into the belief that the working class has interests in common with their employers.[27]

As Kim, a respondent in this study, stated in her narrative, "I wish everybody could have a union." Indeed, strong international unions are needed to offset the deleterious effects of the global economy.

OUTSOURCING AND LIBERTARIANISM

For the women in this study who work in the telecommunications industry, globalization poses at least one major threat. According to a service technician with a local telephone company, craft workers are protected to a certain extent by the necessities of installation, maintenance, and repair of "the facilities or plant," the hardware and infrastructure of the industry. This craft worker, who wishes to remain anonymous, also indicated that his is a beleaguered company, one threatened by the corporate libertarianism that focuses on short-term profits at the expense of the long-term viability of the company to serve its customers. He also compared the telecommunications industry to the power companies in the northeast whose infrastructure failure in 2003 highlighted their lack of investment in hardware and physical structures. "This is a publicly traded company only interested in making money and growth. The quality of services and maintenance of the physical plant are ignored." While the craft workers are likely to be protected, customer service jobs, including operators and directory assistance, are possible targets for globalization in this industry and others. Many service jobs have been outsourced to other countries with English-speaking populations.

Many service, information technology, and clerical jobs in the United States are being outsourced, including banking and government information services. In this study, Ellen, a retired telecommunications worker who now works as a labor activist in North Carolina, spoke of the dangers of outsourcing in her narrative. Naomi Klein notes that this trend creates workers who are no longer loyal and companies that "lose their natural allies among blue-collar workers who have been disenfranchised by callously executed layoffs, sudden mill closures and constant company threats to move offshore."[28] Klein further suggests that today's workers are at the mercy of an "economy that consistently and unapologetically puts profits before people."[29]

TRANSNATIONAL UNIONS

The women in this study who work in the tire manufacturing industry offer a more positive perspective on globalization. These women work for a transnational company that is headquartered in Germany, a country with a high rate of unionization. When the contract that the company had with the United Steel Workers of America (USWA) expired in 1999, negotiations deteriorated over the loss of jobs, overtime rights, and subcontracting issues. The ensuing strike was more than a year in duration, and during this time, the workers learned about the power of the union and the international solidarity with their USWA sisters and brothers in other countries. As Kim notes, "We sent a letter to the parent company in Germany so that the workers there would know what was going on." The USWA also bought enough shares in the company to participate in the stockholder meetings, as Kim says, "to tell the stockholders over there what was happening over here. And that helped a lot." Union members from Germany came to Charlotte to visit with the striking workers and to meet with the union local before addressing company officials. "Everything was in place just about because we had put so much pressure on the [German union]." Another international show of solidarity occurred when tire workers in Africa demonstrated their support. "For one hour one day, everyone stopped work to support our strike, and that was good, too. So that's when we really got [the company's] attention."

In her 2003 essay, "Global Cities and Survival Circuits," Saskia Sassen agrees that working women are caught in the global economic nexus. "Both in global cities and in survival circuits, women emerge as crucial economic actors. It is partly through them that key components of new economies have been built. Globalization allows links to be forged between countries that send migrants and countries that receive them; it also enables local and regional practices to go global."[30] As Mary Margaret Fonow notes in *Union Women*, globalization and the deregulation of trade and labor require that "union feminists . . . build international or transnational forms of feminist solidarity."[31] Writing about women in the USWA, Fonow calls for union feminists to utilize the new networks created by globalization to forge new strength.

> The increasingly transnational political opportunity structures for organized labor and for the women's movement include nontraditional sites for organized politics, such as international law; international labor institutions; nongovernmental organizations (NGOs); the United Nations' tribunals, conferences, and covenants; human rights platforms; and cross-border organizing campaigns.[32]

Global networks can therefore be used in positive ways to support the efforts of organized labor as was seen in the tire manufacturing labor dispute in Charlotte. Union workers in the tire industry around the globe responded to the plight of their fellow workers in the United States, actions which focused attention on the company's unfair practices and eventually forced negotiations to favor the workers. As a result of the strike, no concessions were made by the union, and no jobs were lost.

The assault on working people by greedy corporations is not a new phenomenon. The organizers and activists in the Industrial Workers of the World (IWW) responded to an unfair economic system early in the twentieth century, and today transnational unions may be the only hope for workers in the global economy. Perhaps workers in the current incarnation of the global economy will heed the words penned by IWW member Joe Hill nearly a century ago:

> Workers of the world, awaken!
> Break your chains, demand your rights.
> All the wealth you make is taken
> By exploiting parasites.
> Shall you kneel in deep submission
> From your cradles to your graves?
> Is the height of your ambition
> To be good and willing slaves?
> Arise, ye prisoners of starvation!
> Fight for your own emancipation;
> Arise, ye slaves of every nation
> In One Union Grand.
> Our little ones for bread are crying,
> And millions are from hunger dying;
> The means the end is justifying,
> 'Tis the final stand.[33]

As members of the IWW knew then and the women in the United Steel Workers of America know now, the solidarity of working people can make a difference. Kim, a local USWA leader, states that "Now, when there's a strike, or we know somebody's having a strike, or somebody's trying to organize, we try to back them and help them, cause it helps to have somebody." Kim also says that when corporations begin to take away workers' rights and benefits, the workers must resist. "[The strike] let me know that if you fight, you *have* to fight. . . . You *shouldn't* have to fight, but you do when you work with companies like this." To combat the job losses, pay cuts, and benefits reductions caused by globalization, workers will be required to oppose the unchecked avarice of companies and to demand renewed protection from legislators. To protect poor and working-class people from the global assault by corporate libertarians, the fabric of hope and resistance must be woven from strong transnational labor unions.

Notes

NOTES TO CHAPTER ONE

1. Bureau of Labor Statistics, "Union Members Summary," n.p.
2. Bureau of Labor Statistics, "Union Affiliation," n.p.
3. Minchin, *Fighting against the Odds*, 183.
4. Salmond, *Gastonia 1929*, 72–74.
5. Yellen, *American Labor Struggles*, 318.
6. Ibid.
7. Ibid., 319.
8. Lewis, "North Carolina at the Cross-roads," 37.
9. Lewis, *Cheap and Contented Labor*, 15.
10. Ibid., 32.
11. Lewis, "North Carolina at the Cross-roads," 47.
12. Frankel, "'Jesus Leads Us, Cooper Needs Us, the Union Feeds Us,'" 112.
13. Minchin, 69.
14. Frankel, 103.
15. Pope, *Millhands and Preachers*, 236–37.
16. Ibid., 201.
17. Hall and others, *Like a Family*, 221.
18. Ibid.
19. Ibid.
20. Frankel, 115.
21. Ibid., 116.
22. Aronowitz, *False Promises*, 215.
23. Butler, *The Psychic Life of Power*, 124.
24. Ibid., 40.
25. Rifkin, *Biosphere Politics*, 229.
26. Ibid.
27. Ibid., 230.
28. Ibid., 231.
29. Gilligan, *In a Different Voice*, xi.
30. Ibid.

31. Ibid., xvi.
32. Ibid.
33. Ibid., xix.
34. Ibid., xx.
35. Belenky and others, *Women's Ways of Knowing*, 9.
36. Ibid., 15.
37. Ibid., 146.
38. Ibid., 147.
39. Ibid.
40. Olsen, *Silences*, 6.
41. Ibid., 10.
42. Ibid., 142–51.
43. MacKendrick, *Immemorial Silence*, 87.
44. Soelle, *The Silent Cry*, 74.
45. Arendt, *The Human Condition*, 193.
46. Gilligan, xi.
47. Sontag, "The Aesthetics of Silence," 15.
48. Ibid.
49. Taylor and others, *Voice and Silence*, 197.
50. Spivak, "Can the Subaltern Speak?," 29.
51. Ibid., 32.
52. Ibid., 33.
53. Spelman, *Fruits of Sorrow*, 168.
54. Estes, *The Gift of Story*, 4–5.
55. Ibid., 30.
56. Lorde, "Age, Race, Class, and Sex," 366.
57. Ibid.

NOTES TO CHAPTER TWO

1. Kleinman and Copp, *Emotions and Fieldwork*, 1. Reprinted by permission of Sage Publications, Inc.
2. Ibid., 7.
3. Ibid., 3.
4. Ibid., 10.
5. Ibid., 12.
6. Ibid., 13.
7. Ibid., 28.
8. Ibid., 31.
9. Jones, *Mama Learned Us to Work*, 4.
10. Casey, *I Answer with My Life*, 213.
11. Weedon, *Feminist Practice and Poststructuralist Theory*, 85.
12. Byerly, *Hard Times Cotton Mill Girls*, 5.
13. Ibid., 6.
14. Ibid., 164.
15. Korstad, *Civil Rights Unionism*, 3.

16. Ibid., 10.
17. Ibid., 419.
18. Fink, *The Maya of Morganton*, 201.
19. Linkon and Russo, *Steeltown USA*, 3.
20. Ibid., 245.
21. Honey, *Black Workers Remember*, 2.
22. Ibid., xxi.
23. Cobble, *Dishing It Out*, xii.
24. Portelli, *The Death of Luigi Trastulli*, 30.
25. Ibid., 31.
26. Ibid., 32.
27. Ibid., 43.
28. Ibid., 70.
29. Ibid.
30. Baxter and Montgomery, *Relating: Dialogues and Dialectics*, 13.
31. Casey, 219.
32. Jensen, "The Silent Psychology," 203–4. Reprinted with permission from The Feminist Press.
33. Ibid., 204.
34. Ibid., 204–5.
35. Ibid., 211.
36. Ibid., 211.
37. Ibid.
38. Anderson, "Beginning Where We Are," 95.
39. Ibid., 99.
40. Ibid., 105.
41. Taylor and others, *Between Voice and Silence*, 35.
42. Ibid., 36.
43. Ibid.
44. Ibid.
45. Oakley, "Interviewing Women," 41.
46. Ibid., 44.
47. Ibid., 47.
48. Ibid., 56.
49. Ibid., 58.
50. Taylor and others, 172.
51. Ibid.
52. Morrison, "1993 Nobel Lecture," n.p.
53. Egan, "The Drowned and the Saved," 99.
54. Ibid., 111.
55. Taylor and others, 173.
56. Gill, *Rhetoric and Human Understanding*, 215.

NOTES TO CHAPTER THREE

1. Arendt, *Crises of the Republic*, 143.

2. Wilson, "Gender Wage Gap," n.p. *The Progressive.* Reprinted by permission from The Progressive Media Project, 409 E. Main St, Madison, WI 53703 www.progressive.org
3. Ibid.
4. National Committee on Pay Equity, 195. Reprinted by permission of National Committee on Pay Equity.
5. Bravo and Santa Anna, "Overview," 191.
6. Ibid., 189.
7. Ibid., 189–90.
8. AAUW, *Women at Work*, 20.
9. Whealin, "Sexual Harassment," 411.
10. Ibid.
11. Baxandall and Gordon, *America's Working Women*," 335.
12. Ibid., 336.
13. Ibid.
14. Ibid.
15. Ibid., 324.
16. Bravo and Santa Anna, 229.
17. Kessler-Harris, *Women Have Always Worked*, 86.
18. Ibid., 162.

NOTES TO CHAPTER FOUR

1. Korstad, *Civil Rights Unionism*, 14–15.
2. Ibid., 14.
3. Ibid., 15.
4. Ibid., 16.
5. Ibid.
6. Ibid., 17.
7. Ibid., 18.
8. Ibid., 21.
9. Thompson, "What Is This IWW?," v.
10. Baxandall and Gordon, *America's Working Women*, 178.
11. Ibid., 181.
12. Ibid., 177.
13. "Elizabeth Gurley Flynn," n.p.
14. Flynn, "Patriotism," n.p.
15. Flynn, "Mine Eyes Have Seen the Glory," n.p.
16. Vorse, "Lawrence Strike," n.p.
17. Flynn, "Memories of the IWW," n.p.
18. Ibid.
19. Baxandall and Gordon, 99.
20. Ibid.
21. Kessler-Harris, 66.
22. Baxandall and Gordon, 99.
23. Ibid., 100.

24. Ibid.
25. Ibid., 102.
26. Ibid., 99.
27. Ibid., 102.

NOTES TO CHAPTER FIVE

1. Tong, *Feminine and Feminist Ethics*, 122.
2. Ibid., 125.
3. Ibid.
4. Ibid., 128.
5. Ibid.
6. Ibid., 116.
7. Ibid., 80.
8. Ibid., 86.
9. Ibid., 102.
10. Ibid., 104.
11. Patterson, "Suffering," 166.
12. Ibid., 167.
13. Pope, *Millhands and Preachers*, 260.
14. Salmond, *Gastonia 1929*, 129.
15. Ibid., 130.
16. Ibid.
17. Ibid., 131.
18. Vorse, *Strike!*, 3.
19. Ibid., 4.
20. Ibid., 17.
21. Ibid., 183.
22. Ibid., 11.
23. Ibid., 118–19.
24. Ibid., 202.
25. Ibid.
26. Ibid., 183.
27. Ibid., 188.
28. Ibid., 203.
29. Ibid.
30. Baker, *In a Generous Spirit*, 49.
31. Ibid., 50.
32. Ibid., 60.
33. Page, *Gathering Storm*, 83.
34. Ibid., 225.
35. Ibid.,336.
36. Ibid., 360.
37. Lumpkin, *To Make My* Bread, 21.
38. Ibid., 29.
39. Liefermann, *Crystal Lee*, 7.

40. Ibid., 19.
41. Ibid., 96.
42. Ibid.
43. Ibid.
44. Ibid., 97.
45. Ibid.
46. Ibid., 109.
47. Ibid., 110.
48. Ibid., 111.
49. Ibid., 131.
50. Ibid., 150.
51. Ibid., 170.

NOTES TO CHAPTER SIX

1. Balser, *Sisterhood and Solidarity*, 25.
2. Greene, *The Dialectic of Freedom*, 116.
3. Balser, 6.
4. Ibid., 5.
5. Ibid., 16.
6. hooks, *Feminist Theory*, 100.
7. Dall, *Women's Rights to Labor*, 78.
8. Ibid., 80.
9. Enstad, *Ladies of Labor*, 73.
10. Ibid.
11. Ibid., 87–88.
12. Bromley, "Feminism and Nonviolent Revolution," 150–51.
13. Ibid.
14. Leghorn, "Economic Roots of the Violent Male Culture," 199.
15. Bravo, "Going Public," 229.
16. Braunstein and others, "What Do Unions Do for Women?," 224.
17. Ibid., 225.
18. Lichtenstein and others, 372–73.
19. Ibid., 448.
20. Ibid.
21. Ibid., 449.
22. Ibid., 450.
23. Balser, 25.
24. Ibid.
25. Ibid., 226.
26. Ibid.
27. Braunstein and others, 226–27.
28. Kaminski, "Teaching Leadership to Union Women," 71.
29. Ibid.
30. Ibid., 71.
31. Fonow, *Union Women*, 82.

32. Kokopeli and Lakey, *Leadership for Change*, 2.
33. Belenky, *Women's Ways of Knowing*, 141.
34. Ibid.
35. Enstad, 87.
36. Greene, 116.
37. Masterson, "Feminist Leaders Can't Walk on Water," 33.
38. AAUW, *Global Voices for Gender Equity*, 44–45.
39. Casey, *I Answer with My Life*, 213.
40. Fonow, *Union Women*, 189.
41. Ibid.
42. Ibid., 190.
43. Ibid.
44. hooks, *Feminism*, 43.
45. Gearhart, "The Future—If There Is One—Is Female," 271.
46. Balser, 16.

NOTES TO CHAPTER SEVEN

1. Samuelson, "The Creaky Job Machine," 46.
2. Burkins, "Politicians Neglect South's Textile Crisis."
3. Lunan, "Town's Foundation Crumbles."
4. Korten, *When Corporations Rule the World*, 123.
5. Ibid., 3.
6. Ibid., 5.
7. Hall and others, *Like a Family*, 81.
8. Korten, 131.
9. Ibid.
10. Ibid., 132.
11. Klein, *No Logo*, 223.
12. Ibid., 223–24.
13. Mishel and others, *The State of Working America 2002–2003*, 190.
14. Bureau of Labor Statistics. "Union Affiliation."
15. Ehrenreich, *Nickled and Dimed*, 210.
16. Saker.
17. Ibid.
18. Smith, "PACE International Union Strike Ends."
19. *Uprising of '34*, 2.
20. Ibid., 3.
21. Ibid., 29.
22. Ibid., 28.
23. Ehrenreich, 144.
24. Ibid., 145.
25. Klein, 224.
26. Ibid., 225.
27. *IWW Songs*.
28. Klein, 266.

29. Ibid., 267.
30. Sassen, "Global Cities and Survival Circuits," 274.
31. Fonow, *Union* Women, 14.
32. Ibid.
33. Kornbluh, *Rebel Voices*, 143.

Bibliography

American Association of University Women. *Global Voices for Gender Equity: How Women Create Change*. Washington, DC: AAUW Educational Foundation, 2003.

American Association of University Women. "Women at Work: Changes and Challenges." *AAUW Outlook*. Vol. 97. No. 1. Spring/Summer 2003. 18–23.

Anderson, Kathryn, Susan Armitage, Dana Jack and Judith Wittner. "Beginning Where We Are: Feminist Methodology in Oral History." In *Feminist Research Methods*. Edited by J. Nielsen. Boulder: Westview Publishing Company, 1990. 94–112.

Arendt, Hannah. *The Human Condition. 2nd Edition*. Chicago: University of Chicago Press, 1998.

———. *Crises of the Republic: Lying in Politics, Civil Disobedience, On Violence, Thoughts on Politics and Revolution*. New York: Harcourt, Brace and Company, 1972.

Aronowitz, Stanley. *From the Ashes of the Old: American Labor and America's Future*. Boston: Houghton Mifflin Company, 1998.

Baker, Christina Looper. *In a Generous Spirit: A First-Person Biography of Myra Page*. Urbana: University of Illinois Press, 1996.

Balser, Diane. *Sisterhood and Solidarity: Feminism and Labor in Modern Times*. Boston: South End Press, 1987.

Baxandall, Rosalyn, and Linda Gordon, Eds. *America's Working Women: A Documentary History, 1660 to the Present*. New York: WW Norton Company, 1995.

Baxter, Leslie A. and Barbara M. Montgomery. *Relating: Dialogues and Dialectics*. New York: Guilford Press, 1996.

Belenky, Mary, and Blythe M. Clinchy, Nancy R. Goldberger, and Jill M. Tarule. *Women's Ways of Knowing: The Development of Self, Voice, and Mind*. New York: Basic Books, 1986.

Blum, F.H. "Getting Individuals to Give Information to the Outsider." In *Qualitative Methodology: Firsthand Involvement with the Social World*. Edited by W. Fistead. Chicago: Markham Publishing Company, 1970. 83–89.

Bravo, Ellen. "Going Public." 1992. In *Women: Images and Realities*. Edited by Amy Kesselman, Lily D. McNair, and Nancy Schniedewind. Mountain View, CA: Mayfield Publishing Company. 1998. 229.

Bravo, Ellen and Gloria Santa Anna. "An Overview of Women and Work." 1998. In *Women: Images and Realities*. Edited by Amy Kesselman, Lily D. McNair, and Nancy Schniedewind. Mountain View, CA: Mayfield Publishing Company. 1998. 189–193.

Braunstein, Jill, Lois Shaw, and Robin Dennis. "What Do Unions Do for Women?" 1994. In *Women: Images and Realities*. Edited by Amy Kesselman, Lily D. McNair, and Nancy Schniedewind. Mountain View, CA: Mayfield Publishing Company, 1998. 224–227.

Bromley, Marion. "Feminism and Nonviolent Revolution." In *Reweaving the Web of Life: Feminism and Nonviolence*. Edited by Pam McAllister. Philadelphia: New Society Press, 1982. 143–155.

Bureau of Labor Statistics. "Union Affiliation of Employed Wage and Salary Workers by State." http://www.bls.gov/news.release/union2.t05.htm (accessed June 6, 2006).

———. "Union Members Summary." http://www.bls.gov/news.release/union2.nr0.htm (accessed June 6, 2006).

Burkins, Glenn. "Politicians Neglect South's Textile Crisis." *Charlotte Observer*. Carolinas ed.: F3. March 31, 2002.

Butler, Judith. *The Psychic Life of Power*. Stanford: Stanford University Press, 1997.

Byerly, Victoria. *Hard Times Cotton Mill Girls: Personal Histories of Womanhood and Poverty in the South*. Ithaca, NY: ILR Press, 1986.

Casey, Kathleen. *I Answer with My Life: Life Histories of Women Teachers Working for Social Change*. New York: Routledge, 1993.

Clark, Daniel J. *Like Night and Day: Unionization in a Southern Mill Town*. Chapel Hill: University of North Carolina Press, 1997.

Cobble, Dorothy Sue. *Dishing It Out: Waitresses and Their Unions in the Twentieth Century*. Urbana: University of Illinois Press, 1991.

Dall, Caroline. *Women's Right to Labor*. In *America's Working Women: A Documentary History, 1660 to the Present*. Edited by Rosalyn Baxandall and Linda Gordon. New York: WW Norton Company, 1995. 78–80.

Egan, Susanna. "The Drowned and the Saved: Primo Levi and Paul Steinberg in Dialogue." *History and Memory*. Volume 13, Number 2. Fall/Winter 2001. 96–112.

Ehrenreich, Barbara. *Nickel and Dimed: On (Not) Getting By in America*. New York: Metropolitan Books, 2001.

"Elizabeth Gurley Flynn." http://www.marxists.org/glossary/people/f/l.htm (accessed December 31, 2003).

Enstad, Nan. *Ladies of Labor, Girls of Adventure*. New York: Columbia University Press, 1999.

Estes, Clarissa Pinkola. *The Gift of Story: A Wise Tale about What Is Enough*. New York: Ballantine Books, 1993.

Fink, Leon. *The Maya of Morganton: Work and Community in the Nuevo New South*. Chapel Hill: University of North Carolina Press, 2003.

Frankel, Linda. "'Jesus Leads Us, Cooper Needs Us, the Union Feeds Us': The 1958 Harriet-Henderson Textile Strike." In *Hanging by a Thread: Social Change in Southern Textiles*. Edited by Jeffrey Leiter, Michael Schulman, and Rhonda Zingraff. Ithaca, NY: ILR Press, 1991. 101–120.

Flynn, Elizabeth Gurley. "Do You Believe in Patriotism?" http://www.marxists. org/subject/women/authors/flynn/1916/patriotism.htm (accessed December 31, 2003).

———. "Memories of the IWW." http://www.lucyparsonsproject.org/iww/flynn_ memories_of_iww.html (accessed 21 Apr. 2006.)

———. "Mine Eyes Have Seen the Glory." http://www.marxists.org/subject/may-day/articles/glory.html (accessed December 31, 2003).

Fonow, Mary Margaret. *Union Women: Forging Feminism in the United Steel-workers of America*. Minneapolis: University of Minnesota Press, 2003.

Gearhart, Sally Miller. "The Future—If There Is One—Is Female." In *Reweaving the Web of Life: Feminism and Nonviolence*. Edited by Pam McAllister. Philadelphia: New Society Press, 1982. 266–285.

Gill, Ann. *Rhetoric and Human Understanding*. Prospect Heights, IL: Waveland Press, 1994.

Gilligan, Carol. *In a Different Voice: Psychological Theory and Women's Development*. Cambridge: Harvard University Press, 1982.

Greene, Maxine. *The Dialectic of Freedom*. New York: Teachers College Press, 1988.

Hall, Jacquelyn, James Leloudis, Robert Korstad, Mary Murphy, Lu Ann Jones, and Christopher Daly. *Like a Family: The Making of a Southern Cotton Mill World*. Chapel Hill: University of North Carolina Press, 1987.

Honey, Michael. *Black Workers Remember: An Oral History of Segregation, Unionism, and the Freedom Struggle*. Berkeley: University of California Press, 1999.

hooks, bell. *Feminism Is for Everybody: Passionate Politics*. Cambridge: South End Press, 2000.

———. *Feminist Theory: From Margin to Center*. Cambridge: South End Press, 1999.

IWW Songs. Chicago: Kerr Publishing Company, 1986 (reprint of 1923 edition.)

Jensen, Barbara. "The Silent Psychology." *Women's Studies Quarterly: Working Lives and Cultures*, Volume XXVI, Numbers 1 & 2. Spring/Summer 1998. 202–215.

Jones, Lu Ann. *Mama Learned Us to Work: Farm Women in the New South*. Chapel Hill: University of North Carolina Press, 2002.

Kaminski, Michelle. "Teaching Leadership to Union Women: The Use of Stories." *Labor Studies Journal*. Summer 2003. Vol. 28, No. 2. 67–77.

Kessler-Harris, Alice. *Women Have Always Worked: A Historical Overview*. New York: Feminist Press, 1971.

Klein, Naomi. *No Logo*. New York: Picador USA, 2002.

Kleinman, Sherryl, and Martha A. Copp. *Emotions and Fieldwork*. Newbury Park, CA: Sage Publications, 1993.

Kokopeli, Bruce, and George Lakey. *Leadership for Change: Toward a Feminist Model*. Santa Cruz, CA: New Society Press, n.d.

Kornbluh, Joyce L., Ed. *Rebel Voices: An IWW Anthology*. Chicago: Kerr Publishing Company, 1998.

Korstad, Robert R. *Civil Rights Unionism: Tobacco Workers and the Struggle for Democracy in the Mid-Twentieth Century South*. Chapel Hill: University of North Carolina Press, 2003.

Korten, David C. *When Corporations Rule the World*. Bloomfield, CT: Kumerian Press, 2001.

Leghorn, Lisa. "The Economic Roots of the Violent Male Culture." In *Reweaving the Web of Life: Feminism and Nonviolence*. Edited by Pam McAllister. Philadelphia: New Society Press, 1982. 195–199.

Leifermann, Henry P. *Crystal Lee: A Woman of Inheritance*. New York: Macmillan Publishing Company, 1975.

Lewis, Nell Battle. "North Carolina at the Cross-Roads." *The Virginia Quarterly Review*. January 1930. 37–47.

Lewis, Sinclair. *Cheap and Contented Labor: The Picture of a Southern Mill Town in 1929*. Scripps-Howard Newspapers, 1929.

Linkon, Sherry Lee and John Russo. *Steeltown USA: Work and Memory in Youngstown*. Lawrence: University Press of Kansas, 2002.

Lumpkin, Grace. *To Make My Bread*. Urbana: University of Illinois Press, 1995.

Lunan, Charles. "Town's Foundation Crumbles." *Charlotte Observer*. Carolinas ed.: 11A. March 24, 2002.

MacKendrick, Karmen. *Immemorial Silence*. Albany: State University of New York Press, 2001.

Masterson, Lorraine. "Feminist Leaders Can't Walk on Water." *Quest*. Spring 1976, 30–33.

Minchin, Timothy. *Fighting Against the Odds: A History of Southern Labor Since World War II*. Gainesville: University Press of Florida, 2004.

Mishel, Lawrence, Jared Bernstein, and Heather Boushey. *The State of Working America 2002–2003*. Ithaca, NY: ILR Press, 2003.

Morrison, Toni. *1993 Nobel Lecture*. http://gos.sbc.edu/m/morrisont.html (accessed February 2, 2003).

National Committee on Pay Equity. "The Wage Gap: Myths and Facts." 1997. In *Women: Images and Realities*. Edited by Amy Kesselman, Lily D. McNair, and Nancy Schniedewind. Mountain View, CA: Mayfield Publishing Company, 1998. 193–200.

Oakley, Ann. "Interviewing Women: A Contradiction in Terms." *Doing Feminist Research*. Edited by H. Roberts. New York: Routledge, 1983. 30–61.

Olsen, Tillie. *Silences*. New York: Delacourte Press, 1978.

Page, Dorothy Myra. *Gathering Storm: A Story of the Black Belt*. New York: International Publishers, 1932.

Patterson, Eleanora. "Suffering." In *Reweaving the Web of Life: Feminism and Nonviolence*. Edited by Pam McAllister. Philadelphia: New Society Press, 1982. 165–174.

Pope, Liston. *Millhands and Preachers: A Study of Gastonia*. New Haven, CT: Yale University Press, 1942.

Portelli, Alessandro. *The Death of Luigi Trastulli and Other Stories: Form and Meaning in Oral History*. Albany: State University of New York Press, 1991.

Riessman, Catherine Kohler. *Narrative Analysis*. Newbury Park, CA: Sage Publications, 1993.

Rifkin, Jeremy. *Biosphere Politics: A New Consciousness for a New Century*. New York: Crown Publishing Company, 1991.

Saker, Anne. "Mill Closes, Town Reels." *Raleigh News and Observer*. State ed.: 1A+. June 8, 2003.

Salmond, John A. *Gastonia 1929: The Story of the Loray Mill Strike*. Chapel Hill: University of North Carolina Press, 1995.

Samuelson, Robert J. "The Creaky Job Machine." *Newsweek*. September 22, 2003. 46.

Sassen, Saskia. "Global Cities and Survival Circuits." In *Global Woman: Nannies, Maids, and Sex Workers in the New Economy*. Edited by Barbara Ehrenreich and Arlie R. Hochschild. New York: Metropolitan Books, 2002. 254–274.

Smith, Robert. "PACE International Union Strike Ends at Ecusta Plant in North Carolina." 16 November 2001. 1–4. http://www.paceunion.org/ecusta. htm (accessed June 2, 2003).

Sontag, Susan. "The Aesthetics of Silence." *Styles of Radical Will*. New York: Dell Publishing Company, 1966. 3–34.

Spivak, Gayatri Chakravorty. "Can the Subaltern Speak?" In *The Post-Colonialist Studies Reader, 2nd Edition*. Edited by Bill Ashcroft, Gareth Griffths, and Helen Tiffin. New York: Routledge, 2005. 28–37.

Taylor, Jill M., Carol Gilligan and Amy Sullivan. *Between Voice and Silence: Women Girls, Race and Relationship*. Cambridge: Harvard University Press, 1995.

Tong, Rosemary. *Feminine and Feminist Ethics*. Belmont, CA: Wadsworth Publishing Company, 1993.

Tucker, A.W. *Ecusta History—1938–1980*. Brevard, NC: Ecusta Paper Company, 1980.

The Uprising of '34. Directors Judith Hefland, George Stoney and Susanne Rostock. Videocassette. PBS. 1995. Transcript.

Vorse, Mary Heaton. "Lawrence Strike." http://www.marx.org/subject/women/ authors/vorse/ lawrence.html (accessed December 31, 2003).

———. *Strike!* Urbana: University of Illinois Press, 1991.

Weedon, Chris. *Feminist Practice and Poststructuralist Theory*. Malden, MA: Blackwell Publishing Company, 1987.

Whealin, Julia. "Sexual Harassment: An Overview of Its Impact for Women." In *Women: Images and Realities*. Edited by Amy Kesselman, Lily D. McNair, and Nancy Schniedewind. Mountain View, CA: Mayfield Publishing Company, 1998. 411–415.

Wilson, Marie. "Study Shows Gender Wage Gap Has Widened." *The Progressive*. December 17, 2003. http://www.progressive.org/mediaproject03/mpwd1703. html (accessed April 23, 2006).

Yellen, Samuel. *American Labor Struggles*. New York: Harcourt, Brace and Company, 1936.

Index

For Product Safety Concerns and Information please contact our EU
representative GPSR@taylorandfrancis.com Taylor & Francis Verlag GmbH,
Kaufingerstraße 24, 80331 München, Germany

Printed and bound by CPI Group (UK) Ltd, Croydon, CR0 4YY

08/05/2025

01864533-0001